DOING IT

GOING AGAINST THE CURRENT

FOLLOWING GOD IN FAITH THROUGH YOUR IMPOSSIBLE

LARRY HUTCHESON

LIFEWISE BOOKS

DOING IT GOD'S WAY SERIES

GOING AGAINST THE CURRENT

FOLLOWING GOD IN FAITH THROUGH YOUR IMPOSSIBLE

LARRY HUTCHESON

All scriptures are taken from the NEW INTERNATIONAL VERSION (NIV): Scripture taken from THE HOLY BIBLE, NEW INTERNATIONAL VERSION ®. Copyright© 1973, 1978, 1984, 2011 by Biblica, Inc.™. Used by permission of Zondervan

Published by:

LIFEWISE BOOKS
PO BOX 1072
Pinehurst, TX 77362
LifeWiseBooks.com

To contact the author: LarryHutcheson.com

Print 978-1-958820-48-3
Ebook 978-1-958820-49-0

DEDICATION

This book is dedicated to the people we serve in Angola Africa.
With access to five million acres for agriculture, we will be able
to provide not only jobs but also produce and food for this
country. Fifty percent of all proceeds from this book will go to
fund these projects.

SPECIAL THANKS

To my mom, Letha, who was always
my advocate and protector.

To my wife, Shalene, who has been with me on this journey
and understands what it's like to go against the current and the
difficult challenges it brings.

CONTENTS

INTRODUCTION

GOING AGAINST THE CURRENT

One early morning at the end of April, thousands of people were planning to run in the Oklahoma City marathon that commemorates the 168 people killed in 1995 when the Murrah Federal Building was bombed. Every year, volunteers and runners participate in this race to show that we can each make a difference and change the world.

One year, my wife and I were helping set up the race. Thousands of participants showed up the day before to pick up their registration packs, facilitated by hundreds of volunteers to make this possible. While volunteering, I heard of a young man serving in the military who was running in the half marathon, whom I will call Darren. He was planning to wear his camo field uniform and carry a backpack that weighed 168 pounds to honor every victim of the bombing.

I asked Darren if he had someone to help him get the backpack off and on during the race. His response was, "No, I'm not planning on stopping."

My plan was to run the half marathon, which is 13.1 miles. So I told him, "After I run the race, I will come back and find you and help you with the backpack as you finish."

That morning the temperature was in the fifties. The sea of runners were lining up to start. Darren was in the front of the race with the 168-pound backpack. The gun went off, and the runners began. My newfound goal was to finish the race as quickly as I could so I could help Darren with his goal of carrying the heavy backpack.

The race was going well, and before long, I had found that I was five miles into the race. God began to speak to my heart. He said, "You have run your race. It's time for you to turn around and go help Darren."

I stopped running and turned around, heading away from the desired finish line. The runners were very confused because I was now heading in the opposite direction. People may stop to rest or walk during races, but runners never turn around and go the opposite way from the finish line.

As I weaved back and forth through the crowd, the runners began to say, "You're going the wrong way," and "What are you doing? The finish line is this way."

Going against the current is a lot harder when you are running a race. Every time you get around one person, there's someone else to dodge. As I made it past the runners, the path finally cleared out. I saw a medical tent at mile marker one and asked the team if they had seen a runner in camo with the backpack. They said nobody had come through yet.

About five minutes later, Darren came over the hill, already in a lot of pain, so we had him stop at the medical tent. I found out Darren had forgotten his insoles in his marching boots, and his feet had started to get blisters. I took the insoles out of my shoes and gave them to Darren to use. The medical team told me that that was not a good idea, but I explained that I'm not the one carrying 168 pounds in a backpack and that I would be okay. So Darren and I started running together towards the finish line.

During the race, my job was to carry the water and sports drinks. When he needed to rest, I would help him take off the backpack so he could reset. After a few minutes, he would put the backpack on and return to the race. Even though we were the very last runners in the half marathon, there was a point in the race where we were able to run with those who were running the full marathon. This helped Darren's morale because we were then running with other people, and they were cheering him on.

Never underestimate the value of your encouragement to others. Even in the race of life, we need to be encouraged to keep going. Sometimes life's races don't make sense. We are asked to do things by God that are humanly impossible. We need to know that we are not alone and that with God nothing is impossible.

> *"I can do all this through him who gives me strength."*
> *Philippians 4:13*

As Darren and I got closer to the finish line, we had to separate from the crowd. Those who were running the half marathon had to turn down a different street. Even though the finish line was the same as the full marathon, there were two ways to get there. That path took us away from the other runners.

I noticed that Darren was starting to doubt that he could finish the race. We stopped to rest and took the backpack off. After about five minutes, I asked, "Are you ready to go and finish the race?"

Darren didn't respond. One of the volunteers ran up and asked Darren if he needed medical help. I responded, "He's okay. Darren is going to finish the race."

Darren looked at me puzzled, as if he was thinking, *He really wasn't talking to you.* I grabbed the backpack and said, "Darren let's go." He stood up with his legs shaking. I said, "We're almost there. We can't quit now." I put the backpack on him, and we started walking toward the finish line.

When we could see the finish line, Darren said, "Run ahead and let them know I am coming." When I got to the finish line, I got the announcer's attention, and I told him Darren was on his way.

The announcer with the microphone saw Darren in the distance. He began to announce what Darren was doing and what he had just accomplished. I turned around to run back toward Darren so I could keep encouraging him to the finish line. That day I was the last one to cross the finish line in the half marathon.

When you run the race that God has for you, it's not about finishing first. It's about helping others and taking all the turns that God wants you to take in life. I learned it's about finishing God's way.

WHAT DOES IT MEAN TO GO AGAINST THE CURRENT?

To describe this simply, it is to live your life under pressure. When God laid out the plans for my life, those plans were impossible for me to carry out on my own. I didn't know where the money would come from to fund the dreams. I didn't even know how to accomplish all God had told me to do.

When I turned my life over to God, He told me I would travel the world and preach His gospel and that someday, I would hold crusades all over America to help people come to know Him and His healing power. When I accepted His plan, I started on a journey, going against the current. I would describe it as the story of Peter in the Bible. One night, all of Jesus' disciples were in a boat. They saw a figure out on the water, and all began to scream, thinking it was a ghost walking on the water.

> *"But Jesus immediately said, 'Take courage! It is I. Don't be afraid.' 'Lord, if it's you,' Peter replied, 'tell me to come to you on the water.' 'Come,' he said. Then Peter got down out of the boat, walked on the water and came toward Jesus. But when he saw the wind, he was afraid and, beginning to sink, cried out, 'Lord, save me!' Immediately, Jesus reached out his hand and*

caught him. 'You of little faith,' he said, 'why did you doubt?'" Matthew 14:27-31

When it comes to following God, there is a safer path. Eleven disciples stayed in the boat, and only one man got out of the boat and started going against the current. He had to completely trust God. It was not an easy task, and he would not have been able to accomplish it by himself.

We must keep our eyes on Jesus. I have felt the wind and waves many times on this journey God has me on and have wanted to quit, telling God it's too difficult. I have learned to ignore the wind and waves whether they are debt, impatience, or life's unknowns. I have often asked God for relief from the pressure, but He just reminds me to keep my eyes upon Him.

WHY PRESSURE?

God is cooking something up inside of us. It will take the right kind of pressure to prepare us for all God has planned. If He lets off the pressure too soon, the preparation will not be complete. I believe God is preparing a banquet for the whole world. The people who taste of God's goodness will not understand the sacrifice it took to prepare the food for the banquet. Those who have been under pressure know it all was worth it in the end.

As you continue on your journey, you are going to find yourself up against the winds of life. I want to encourage you—you're not alone. Keep your eyes on Him.

CHAPTER 1

GOD PROMISES

When I was ten years old, my dad was preaching at a church. The worship leader interrupted the service and had me come up to the front. At first, I thought I was in trouble for not paying attention during church. I grew up very hyperactive, and it was hard for me to sit still.

The worship leader said to the pastor, "I want to be obedient to God. God wants us to pray for this little boy, and He wants me to tell him God has a big plan for his life." I didn't understand what this really meant and why they were praying over me.

My mom would continue to tell me as I got older that I didn't belong to her but that I belonged to God, and she was raising me for God's plan. I would tell my mom, "I know what God's plan is; I'm going to play football in the NFL." She would just laugh and say, "Well, just do what He tells you to do."

When God begins to layout His plan for your life, He will start with little things to get you to listen. In the Bible, there is a story of Moses. During the time of his birth, the Egyptian king, Pharoah, was killing all the Hebrew boys from birth to two years old.

> *"The king of Egypt said to the Hebrew midwives, whose names were Shiphrah and Puah, 'When you are helping the Hebrew women during childbirth on the delivery stool, if you see that the baby is a boy kill him; but if it is a girl let her live.'" Exodus 1:15-16*

The midwives feared God and ignored Pharoah's ruling. Then Pharoah questioned the midwives and asked them why they let the boys live.

> *"The midwives answered Pharaoh, 'Hebrew women are not like Egyptian women; they are vigorous and give birth before the midwives arrive.'" Exodus 1:19*

God had a plan for Moses. Even though the Pharaoh issued a ruling to throw all the boys into the Nile, God made a way for Moses to escape. Moses' mother saw the favor of God upon his life and did everything she could to save him. She had planned to put him in a basket and send him down the Nile when Pharaoh's daughter and maidservants went to bathe. God not only saved Moses, but He also put him in Pharaoh's house to be raised by Pharaoh's daughter.

We don't know if Moses' mother believed he would set their people free from slavery, but we do know she saw the favor of God upon his life, and that's all she needed to know. When we follow God, we are responsible to do our part, and God will always follow through with His promises.

GOD'S CALLING AND PROMISES ON MY LIFE

When I was sixteen years old, I was in a car accident. My car flipped over, and I was not wearing my seat belt. I felt like I was being slammed back and forth in my car until it settled on all four wheels. I felt God's presence enter my car, and I began to feel conviction for all the things I was doing for myself and for following my own plan. I heard God say, "I'll give you one more chance." I knew what that meant. I had to start living His plan and not my own.

The following Sunday morning service at church, I heard God's voice again. God had a plan for my life. He wanted me to travel around the world and share His Word. I began to ask God some personal questions about my future. Would I get married and have children before I start traveling? He said, "Yes, you will have a family, and you will know when it is time to go."

I said yes to God's plan. The promise that God gave that morning at church has guided me throughout my life. It has allowed me to have faith in this plan, even when it doesn't make sense in my heart or my mind. Throughout my life, I've learned to trust God's promises. At times, the promises felt so far away and looked as if it would never happen. God has remained faithful to His promise.

MOSES AND THE BURNING BUSH

I believe every person should have a God encounter. God encounters in my life have shown me how powerful God really is. They have developed my belief that God can do anything. Not everybody is called to change the world like Moses.

Nobody can argue with your God encounter. These experiences between God and you help mold and shape you. When we look at Moses and the burning bush, we see the God encounter Moses had that led him back to Egypt to set his people free.

After fleeing from Egypt, Moses found himself in Midian. Moses got married and was now working as a shepherd for his father-in-law, who was the priest of Midian. That day, he led the flock to the far side of the wilderness to Horeb, the mountain of God.

> *"There the angel of the LORD appeared to him in flames of fire from within a bush..." Exodus 3:2*

This God encounter got Moses' attention. It wasn't strange that the bush was on fire, but what got Moses' attention was that the bush did not burn up. God doesn't show up in your life and reveal His power because it would be a cool thing to experience. God doesn't use these encounters so that you will get saved and know that He is real. There is a bigger picture God is trying to reveal.

Moses was having a normal day leading the sheep, but God directed him down a different path to reveal His plan. For Moses, going against the current was to stop being a sheep herder and go rescue his people from slavery. This was an impossible task without God. Moses had no authority of his own to set the people free.

Moses tried to set the people free within his own power by killing an Egyptian who was beating a Hebrew slave. When Pharaoh heard what Moses had done, he tried to have Moses killed. I believe Moses knew he was to set the people free from their slavery but didn't know how to accomplish God's task. So Moses fled to Midian and gave up trying to help his own people become free.

THE CRY OF THE PEOPLE

> "The LORD said, 'I have indeed seen the misery of my people in Egypt. I have heard them crying out because of their slave drivers, and I am concerned about their suffering. So I have come down to rescue them from the land of the Egyptians and to bring them up out of that land into a good and spacious land, a land flowing with milk and honey—the home of the Canaanites, Hittites, Amorites, Perizzites, Hivites and Jebusites. And now the cry of the Israelites has reached me, and I have seen the way of the Egyptians are oppressing them.'" Exodus 3:7-11

GOING AGAINST THE CURRENT

As the Israelites cried out to the Lord, He heard them and saw their misery. When we complain and feel like life is unfair, God will not hear our complaining. Even though the Israelites had endured centuries of slavery, they turned to God for help and trusted in His deliverance. God not only saw their misery but also took notice of how the Egyptians were mistreating them, and He was deeply concerned about their suffering. In response, He made the choice to give them the best of the land and lead them out of Egypt.

When God puts something in your heart to accomplish for Him, He already has the exact day and time in mind. Waiting on God's timing is a big part of accomplishing what God has asked you to do. He knows stepping out and going against the current is hard. As God laid out His plan on how to set the Hebrew people free, there were a lot of unknowns on Moses' part for how it would be accomplished.

> *"But Moses said to God, 'Who am I that I should go to Pharaoh and bring the Israelites out of Egypt?'"*
> *Exodus 3:11*

I have felt this way when God gave me His plan for my life. I thought to myself, *surely there is someone more qualified and a lot smarter than I am.* I have found that God does not see us the same way we see ourselves. I was not asked to go against the current because I was qualified. I have learned that God qualified me through the process of obedience.

When we keep our eyes on Jesus and pay no attention to the wind and waves, that is the simple faith and trust God is

12

looking for. He has asked us to carry out His plan. We don't need to overthink or make sense of what He's asked us to do. The process can be very scary, and it will often look impossible without God's miracles being performed.

One of Moses' concerns were:

> *"What if they do not believe me or listen to me and say, 'The LORD did not appear to you'?" Exodus 4:1*

God gave Moses two miracle signs to perform for Pharaoh and the people. When Moses threw his staff on the ground, it became a snake. Then the LORD said to Moses, "Reach out your hand and take the snake by the tail," and it returned as his staff. The second miracle was when he put his hand inside the cloak. He took his hand out, and his skin had leprosy and had become as white as snow. But when he put his hand back in the cloak, it was restored like the rest of his flesh (Exodus 4:2-7).

When God gives you a promise, His hand will be upon you. He will give you favor to accomplish the task. Even though Moses tried to convince God that he was unqualified and that God should choose someone else, Moses chose to go against the current. He went to his father-in-law and asked him to let him return to his people in Egypt.

> *"…Jethro said, 'Go and I wish you well.'" Exodus 4:18*

MY GOD ENCOUNTER

When I was eighteen years old, the pastor asked me to preach in the evening service. This would be the first time I ever preached in the main sanctuary. I had spoken in the youth service before but never to adults. During the weeks prior, I was planning to dedicate a Saturday to prepare my sermon. However, God woke me up early, which I wasn't very happy about because I had intended to take the whole day for God to give me a message. I didn't see the importance of waking up early, but I got out of bed and decided to fix a big breakfast.

As I started watching TV, I heard the Lord telling me to go pray. Even though I tried to explain to God that I would dedicate the whole Saturday for Him to give me a message, I first wanted to eat my breakfast and watch TV. But I heard God's voice again, "Go pray." Before I could answer back, the TV shut off. I tried to fix it, but the TV repair guy later explained that it had overheated.

Again, I heard God say, "Go pray." So I went into my parents' office and sat at the computer, saying to the Lord, "Okay, I'm ready. You can give me the message You want me to preach." But I heard the voice again, "Go pray!" Then I went to my room and surrendered to God, saying, "Whatever You want to do in me right now, I give You permission."

As I turned on the radio and began to praise the Lord, I felt His presence fill the room. I fell down to the ground and could not move. While lying there with my face down toward the carpet, every time I tried to breathe in, I would suck carpet into my mouth. I had to move my face to the side to breathe.

When God's presence released off me, I could stand up, but I noticed that my neck was hurting. I asked the Lord what had happened, and God said, "I'm very powerful." I believe He was teaching me that He could do anything, and I should never put any limitations on Him. That day changed my life, and I saw God in a different way than ever before. I went from spending twenty minutes a day with the Lord to spending two hours a day with Him. I was so hungry for His presence that two hours seemed to go by fast. I learned there was a big difference between preparing a message and spending time in prayer with my heavenly Father.

When God gives you a promise, it looks different from simply doing something for Him. Carrying something in your heart for God involves a process that must take place before you can act upon it. It involves God's timing and a process to qualify you for different seasons in your life. In my life, I've been carrying a promise for over thirty years.

Despite my apparent success in various areas, such as getting married to my high school sweetheart, raising three accomplished daughters, being in the ministry for decades, and owning businesses, I still feel undone and incomplete. There's a hole in my heart that nothing can fill until I can accomplish what God has told me to do. Waiting on God and trusting in His promises have caused me to die to my dreams and desires and to wait for God's perfect timing.

People who don't understand what you're going through may tell you to just go out and do what God has told you to do. However, when the dream is too big and you cannot accomplish it on your own, all you can do is wait on God. This waiting process is similar to Moses' story; he carried a promise of God but had to wait for God's timing and His way of fulfilling it.

To all those carrying God's promise in their hearts, I want to encourage you not to give up or shrink back but to press on! That day of fulfillment is coming! Remember, the Bible says God will never leave you nor forsake you (Hebrews 13:5). Trust the process; God is using this time to qualify you so you can accomplish all that's in your heart.

CHAPTER 2

THE CURRENT WILL TAKE YOU TO PLACES YOU DON'T WANT TO GO

God is seeking champions of faith in the present day—followers of God who diligently adhere to His instructions to fulfill His tasks. Life's current is often guided by emotions, common sense, and the pursuit of safety. While these factors may not appear negative, they heavily influence people's choices. Decisions like which college they will go to, whom to marry, and where they will live are frequently shaped by these considerations. I'm not suggesting we live recklessly and not try to make good decisions.

In my personal experience, I have found carrying a promise from God requires me to remove fear and doubt while gaining a clear understanding of what God wants me to do. Being a champion for God necessitates going against the current. The Bible provides examples such as David, Moses, and Joseph as well as women like Esther, Ruth, and Hannah. Each of them held promises from God, believing they could do great things for Him. To fulfill these tasks, they had to take leaps of faith.

David, for instance, was promised kingship. Moses was tasked with delivering his people. Joseph was destined for greatness within his family. Esther was promised she would be queen. Ruth received the promise that God would give her a husband and Hannah a child. Throughout this journey, there will be risks and unknowns. You can't play it safe or make sense of it. You either trust the process that God has you in, or you don't.

When you look at the story of David, he would have never fought a 9 ½-foot-tall man if the decision was made from his emotion, common sense, and need for safety. In this story, there was a great war between the Israelites and the Philistines. The Philistines occupied one hill and the Israelites another, with the valley in between.

A champion named Goliath emerged from the Philistine's camp, challenging any Israelite man to fight him. Filled with fear, King Saul and his troops fled at the sight of Goliath. David, the champion of the faith, held a different perspective. He believed in God and His power. As David approached the camp where the soldiers were staying, he heard Goliath's shouts of defiance against Israel.

"David asked the men standing near him, 'What will be done for the man who kills this Philistine and removes this disgrace from Israel? Who is this uncircumcised Philistine that he should defy the armies of the living God?'" 1 Samuel 17:26

David was not worried about his safety or trying to make sense of how he could possibly face this giant. He knew God would deliver him a victory and fulfill the promise of making him King of Israel. When your faith in God is unwavering, the unthinkable becomes achievable.

Part of the process for David to become king was watching his father's flock. Even after he had been anointed by Samuel to become king, David returned to his father's sheep until God had brought David's promise into existence. God used this process to show David that he needed to be full of faith and trust God for his protection.

David had already faced eminent danger when he was guarding the flock. He experienced victory over both a lion and a bear. When it was time to stop being a shepherd and fulfill the plan God had for him, He wasn't scared to face a giant because he had already seen the power of God.

I believe David wasn't afraid to die. He saw this as an opportunity to show how powerful God really was and how to destroy the enemies of God. It didn't matter that Goliath was a giant. He wasn't concerned about his résumé with how many people he had killed on it. He knew what God had promised, and that was good enough for him. David was eager to learn what reward awaited the man who killed this towering giant.

> *"Now the Israelites had been saying... 'The king will give great wealth to the man who kills him. He will also give him his daughter in marriage and will exempt his family from taxes in Israel.'" 1 Samuel 17:25*

Then King Saul heard all that David was saying about the giant and how David could destroy the Philistine. When this was reported to King Saul, he sent for him.

> *"David said to Saul, 'Let no one lose heart on account of this Philistine; your servant will go and fight him.' Saul replied, 'You are not able to go out against this Philistine and fight him; you are only a young man, and he has been a warrior from his youth.' But David said to Saul, 'Your servant has been keeping his father's sheep. When a lion or a bear came and carried off a sheep from the flock, I went after it, struck it and rescued the sheep from its mouth. When it turned on me, I seized it by its hair, struck it and killed it. Your servant has killed both the lion and the bear; this uncircumcised Philistine will be like one of them, because he has defied the armies of the living God. The LORD who rescued me from the paw of the lion and the paw of the bear will rescue me from the hand of this Philistine.'" 1 Samuel 17:32-37*

As David approached the Philistine, he carried nothing but a sling in one hand and five smooth stones he pulled from a nearby stream in the other. David remained true to who he was and didn't try to be somebody else. Rather than attack the giant as a warrior, he confronted him as a shepherd. He had not only seen God protect his flock but attributed the victory for killing the lion and the bear to Him. David's strength was not dependent on his might or power but on his acknowledgment of God's power through him.

> *"David said to the Philistine, 'You come against me with sword and spear and javelin, but I come against you in the name of the LORD Almighty, the God of the armies of Israel, whom you have defied. This day the LORD will deliver you into my hands, and I'll strike you down and cut off your head. This very day I will give the carcasses of the Philistine army to the birds and the wild animals, and the whole world will know that there is a God in Israel. All of those gathered here will know that it is not by sword or spear that the LORD saves; for the battle is the LORD's, and he will give all of you into our hands.'" 1 Samuel 17:45-47*

David gave full credit to God. He didn't come against Goliath with weapons, but David said, "I come against you in the name of the LORD Almighty, the God of the armies of Israel." David's motivation wasn't personal glory, honor, or fame; he aimed to manifest the presence of God when he said, "The whole world will know that there is a God in Israel." David was not depending on the stones to kill Goliath. He knew it would take an act of God. His proclamation echoed, "The battle is the LORD's, and he will give all of you into our hands."

When you don't have direction from God, the current will take you down life's road. Those who think it's just about making enough money or living an easy life will go down paths that are well worn down. They will look for the safe places and familiar routes. Living without God's guidance often subjects you to being led by your emotions, common sense, and pursuit of safety. Rest assured, God has big plans for you that lead to a path less traveled. The journey may have a lot of turns and likely won't allow you to see too far ahead. It will likely seem impossible by yourself because you can't do it on your own. It will take God's ability to accomplish His promises. We must have a vision, or we will perish (Proverbs 29:18).

BE CAREFUL WHAT YOU FOCUS ON

When the Israelites left Egypt, God gave them a promise—a journey to take them to a land flowing with milk and honey. Upon their arrival, instead of seeing the land's richness and abundance, they saw giants. When you focus on the wrong thing you will often miss the purpose. Fear will begin to grip you and stop you from moving forward with God. God already knew about the people who lived in this land. When a mountain is standing in your way, you must know God can remove the mountain. If the mountain captures your focus, you may be overwhelmed and likely go nowhere. But if God has your focus, you can accomplish anything. When the leaders came back and gave their report of the land, they said:

> *"We went into the land to which you sent us, and it does flow with milk and honey! Here is its fruit. But the people who live there are powerful, and the cities are fortified and very large…" Numbers 13:27-28*

Two men named Joshua and Caleb were a part of the twelve men that went over and spied throughout the land.

> *"Then Caleb silenced the people before Moses and said, 'We should go up and take possession of land, for we can certainly do it.'" Numbers 13:30*

When you focus on the right things, like the task at hand rather than the whole mountain, it makes the next right step doable. There isn't room for doubt when the step becomes that simple. The other ten leaders spread a bad report about the land they were to inhabit creating doubt and apprehension among the Israelites. As they focused on the size of the people, the land and its produce became insignificant. For they said:

> *"We seemed like grasshoppers in our own eyes, and we looked the same to them." Numbers 13:33b*

God attempted to prepare the Israelites for what they would face when they went over to spy in the land. He had guided them with a cloud by day and fire by night. He even parted the Red Sea and destroyed the Egyptian armies. In the desert, He gave them water to drink and food to eat.

> *"The LORD said to Moses, 'How long will these people treat me with contempt? How long will they refuse to*

believe in me, in spite of all the signs I have performed among them?'" Numbers 14:11

Because the Israelite people were focusing on the giants, they refused to go to the Promised Land. They began to say it would be better for us to go back to Egypt.

Following God isn't always easy to do. God has asked me to do things I didn't want to do. There have been times when I wanted to take the easy path. I would get excited and think God was going to open a door that would make life easier. I've always worked more than one job and have learned to change hats from job to job. I didn't understand why God had me on this path. I would see others with singular employment and become envious. Now, I recognize what God was doing. Had I grasped the full extent of the commitment these tasks entailed, I doubt I would have eagerly signed up. Looking back, I see how this journey has molded my character, and I am thankful to God for setting it up perfectly for me.

DON'T BE A WANDERER

A person with no direction or vision is doomed to wander. The Israelites serve as an example of what rejecting God's promise can result in—forty years of wandering. Being a wanderer is perhaps one of life's gravest lots. The Israelites wandered around the desert with no destination or plan to get anywhere. God's proclamation echoed with clarity: not a single one of them would set foot in the Promised Land.

"The LORD replied, 'I have forgiven them, as you asked. Nevertheless, as surely as I live and as surely as the glory of the LORD fills the whole earth, not one of those who saw my glory and the signs I performed in Egypt and in the wilderness but who disobeyed me and tested me ten times—not one of them will ever see the land I promised on oath to their ancestors. No one who has treated me with contempt will ever see it. But because my servant Caleb has a different spirit and follows me wholeheartedly, I will bring him into the land he went to, and his descendants will inherit it. Since the Amalekites and the Canaanites are living in the valleys, turn back tomorrow and set out toward the desert along the route to the Red Sea.'"
Numbers 14:20-25

When the Israelite people rejected God, He drew the line. Every person over the age of twenty who had seen the miracles of God and those who had grumbled against the Lord would not see the land God had promised. Their consequence spanned forty years—a year to mirror each day they scouted the land. This period would entail them being held accountable for their transgressions, a firsthand experience of God's adversity.

If at a crossroads you turn away from God's promise and go your own path, you leave God behind either purposefully or inadvertently, and He will no longer be with you. Along my journey, God has cautioned me regarding the dangers of going my own way. When the Israelites decided to go ahead and claim the land on their own, Moses said:

"Why are you disobeying the LORD's command? This will not succeed! Do not go up, because the LORD is not with you. You will be defeated by your enemies, for the Amalekites and the Canaanites will face you there. Because you have turned away from the LORD, he will not be with you and you will fall by the sword. Nevertheless, in their presumption they went up toward the highest point in the hill country, though neither Moses nor the ark of the LORD's covenant moved from the camp. Then the Amalekites and the Canaanites who lived in that hill country came down and attacked them and beat them down all the way to Hormah." Numbers 14:41-45

The Lord will give you direction on your journey. If He says to stop, don't move. If He says go, He will give you direction. The Israelites made their mistake when Moses and the ark of God stayed in their camp. They went on their own way and thus were not protected by God.

TRYING TO SURVIVE ON YOUR OWN

Because of the hardening of the Israelite's hearts toward God, they were forced to try and survive on their own. They were even willing and eager to go back to Egypt and live in slavery. What amazes me about this story is the stark selfishness of the Israelite people. They weren't thinking of their children, and they weren't thinking about God and all He had done for them.

A hardened heart solely focused on trying to survive on your own often leads to these types of mistakes.

When the Israelites were in the desert for forty years, God did not let their clothes wear out. Every morning He gave them manna to eat. When they complained about the manna, He gave them quail. On two separate occasions He gave them water out of a rock. The Lord will be faithful even when people are not.

This narrative contains a strong warning, urging us to stay on the right path and trust the promises of God. God's intent isn't punitive; however, veering off His course carries inherent consequences. If we walk away from the Lord's plan, we fall outside of His protection and will.

CHAPTER 3

GOING IN THE WRONG DIRECTION

Reaching the finish line often means navigating against the current, much like the story I shared earlier about the half marathon. When you are called to do something for God that is bigger than you, the journey can take you on a myriad of paths. When you look at the story of the Israelite people being in the desert for forty years, while most people focus on those who died and didn't make it to the Promised Land, Caleb and all his descendants clung to God's assurance that someday they would cross the Jordan.

FOLLOWING GOD'S DIRECTION WILL GET YOU TO GOD'S PROMISE

During the half marathon, a moment in the race came when God directed me to pivot and assist another runner; I had already run my race. The runners noticing that I was going in the wrong direction must've been how people looked at the Israelites when they turned around and went back into the desert for forty years. During this prolonged journey, Caleb and Joshua had to remember what God promised, especially amidst different fatal plagues and biting snakes.

I believe the promise of God keeps us going. We cannot be distracted by things around us. When we have a promise from God, we must keep moving to our destination.

Upon Moses' passing, God charged Joshua, declaring, "My servant is dead. So get ready to cross the Jordan River into the land I'm about to give to you and to the Israelite people. I will also give you every place where you set your foot, as I have promised Moses." When I was in my twenties, I mistakenly believed that divine directives translated into effortless achievement. The Lord, however, knew the journey would be hard. Same with the Israelites. They would have to have faith in God's promises to accomplish claiming the land. The Lord said:

> *"Be strong and courageous, because you will lead these people to inherit the land I swore to their ancestors to give them. Be strong and very courageous. Be careful to obey all the law my servant Moses gave you; do not turn from it to the right or to the left, that you may be*

successful wherever you go. Keep this Book of the Law always on your lips; meditate on it day and night, so that you may be careful to do everything written in it. Then you will be prosperous and successful. Have I not commanded you? Be strong and courageous. Do not be afraid; do not be discouraged, for the LORD your God will be with you wherever you go." Joshua 1:6-9

Three times the Lord told Joshua, "Be strong and courageous." The journey will not be easy, and doing things for God necessitates unwavering trust and faith. The Lord is not looking for weak people; thus, we must remove all doubt and fear. There are people all around us who are lost and don't know the way to the Lord, and I am convinced God seeks individuals who will unhesitatingly follow Him into dangerous places to pull people out of the clutches of hell.

As Joshua readied the people to go take the land God had promised, he gathered his officers, instructing them to prepare provisions for crossing the Jordan and take possession of the land. Through their journey, the people learned to do what God said and not to question His plans. They remembered how their predecessors had disobeyed God. I often wondered how the Bible might have read if their elders had trusted God and went to the Promised Land with Moses. Sometimes people just don't operate in faith and when fear grips their heart, they will ignore God's perfect plan.

Yet, we can learn from our past and not allow it to define us. Thank God for His mercy. Even when we mess up, God gives us another path to the finish line. The Israelites, not raised in slavery but rather in the wilderness for forty years, gradually learned to trust God.

> *"Then they answered Joshua, 'Whatever you have commanded us we will do, and wherever you send us we will go. Just as we fully obeyed Moses, so we will obey you. Only may the LORD your God be with you as he was with Moses. Whoever rebels against your word and does not obey it, whatever you may command them, will be put to death. Only be strong and courageous!'" Joshua 1:16-18*

The people became united as one body with a shared purpose. The Israelites were willing to follow Joshua, even as they followed Moses. When Moses was up in the mountain talking with God, He had given him the Ten Commandments. The people of Israel began to turn away from God because Moses had been gone for a while on the mountain. The leaders decided to make a golden calf to worship and even declared that this idol set them free from Egypt. When Moses came down and saw the people worshipping, dancing, and singing to the golden calf, he became angry and destroyed the tablets of the Ten Commandments. Moses drew a line and called for those who were for God to come on one side of the line and then he declared that all the people who were in rebellion were to be killed. This looks very harsh that God would request this of Moses and the people that were going to serve the Lord, but wicked people will lead you astray.

We must grasp the reality that not everyone chooses to head in God's direction and be careful who we partner with on this journey because they can lead us off course. We are not supposed to kill people because they disagree with God like back in Joshua's day, but it is crucial to distance ourselves from people who could derail our course and keep us from moving toward our finish line.

DON'T QUIT IN THE MIDDLE OF THE RACE

When I mention our finish line, I'm not talking about at the end of our life or when we go to heaven. Our lives are composed of many races with numerous finish lines. Personally, the thought of starting a race and not finishing is scary. If you quit, you will be stuck in that race and not able to move on in your life and be searching for meaning and purpose indefinitely. I'm grateful I've never quit on God's plans. I have felt like quitting, but I have learned from others that quitting will leave you with no direction with God.

We see Joshua and the Israelites going into the Promised Land with their finish line being the Jordan River. God led them back to the very territory the elders, who were not willing to cross the Jordan River, encountered forty years prior. The Israelite people crossed this important finish line and saw the hand of God was with them the entire way.

When Joshua sent over two spies, he issued a clear directive: scout the land with a particular focus on Jericho. The spies ventured out, finding refuge in the house of a prostitute named Rahab.

It was on her roof under the stocks of flax, where there they sought to hide. Even though Rahab was a prostitute, God sent the two spies to her home to be protected. Many people harbor judgment and doubt regarding certain individuals' ability to be used by God.

Though Rahab led a life of sin, she had heard about the God of Israel. Rahab feared the reports she had heard, so when the two spies came to her for refuge, she protected them from her own people. No matter how badly we have sinned, the Lord can still change our lives. In shielding the spies and facilitating their escape, Rahab exemplified courage and obedience to God.

> *"Before the spies lay down for the night, she went up on the roof and said to them, 'I know that the LORD has given you this land and that a great fear of you has fallen on us, so that all who live in this country are melting in fear because of you. We have heard how the LORD dried up the water of the Red Sea for you when you came out of Egypt, and what you did to Sihon and Og, the two kings of the Amorites east of the Jordan, whom you completely destroyed. When we heard of it, our hearts melted in fear and everyone's courage failed because of you, for the LORD your God is God in heaven above and on the earth below.'" Joshua 2:8-11*

The two spies laid out a plan to protect Rahab and all her family.

> *"Now the men had said to her, 'This oath you made us swear will not be binding on us unless, when we enter the land, you have tied this scarlet cord in the window*

through which you let us down, and unless you have brought your father and mother, your brothers and all your family into your house. If any of them go outside your house in the street, their blood will be on their own heads; we will not be responsible. As for those who are in the house with you, their blood will be on our head if a hand is laid on them. But if you tell what we are doing, we will be released from the oath you made us swear. Joshua 2:17-20

Early in the morning, Joshua and all the Israelites set out to cross the Jordan. The people were instructed to follow the Ark of God while maintaining a certain amount of distance from it. This space underscored the holiness of the Ark while reinforcing the knowledge that God was with them. This visual signified that God was going before them, so they didn't have to fear. They knew He would drive their enemies out of their designated inheritance before them.

The priest was called to carry the Ark of God. Joshua appointed twelve men, one from each of the tribes, to undertake this sacred responsibility. As the Ark of God entered the waters of the Jordan, a miracle occurred—the flow of water came to a halt.

"The priest who carried the ark of the covenant of the Lord stopped in the middle of the Jordan and stood on dry ground, while all Israelite passed by until the whole nation had completed the crossing on dry ground." Joshua 3:17

REVEALING THE POWER

As God revealed His power at the Jordan River, He is able to show His power to the world. As His children, we must not be afraid to introduce God and all His promises. His Word says that He is the same yesterday, today, and always. He has not changed; He still reveals His power by saving the lost and healing the sick. God has not run out of power, and we must trust Him to show up in our greatest needs.

I have encountered people who were desperate for a display of God's power. They had received a doctor's report that they were going to die in six months, and there was nothing that could be done. Cancer had spread throughout their entire body. I was at the hospital when the doctor was talking to a friend of mine. The doctor's report was that this patient had a twenty percent chance to live because of the type of cancer.

Doctors are men and women trained to help people with illnesses and sicknesses, and God isn't against doctors or medicine. We must acknowledge not only the diversity of individuals and their beliefs in God but also that we are not all destined to die the same way.

In the hallway, outside my friend's room, I waited, uncertain of the doctor's next words but steadfast in knowing God had the answer. When the doctor left her room, I walked back in, and she had a smile on her face. I asked her what the doctor said?

She said, "I have six months to live."

I knew she believed God would heal her. So I took her by the hand and said, "God will release His power out of my hand. Hold it as long as you need to."

As she held my hand for about forty-five minutes, I felt the power of God releasing into her body. God showed up in a big way! She didn't die in six months or a year because God healed her of cancer. She was able to go back home and live a healthy life.

As we continue observing the journey of Joshua crossing the Jordan with the Ark of God leading them, once their feet hit the other side of the Jordan, the waters begin to flow again. God demonstrated His power again at the finish line.

YOUR NEXT RACE IS ALREADY PLANNED

Life will present many races. Each will have a beginning and an end. God uses each race to prepare us for the next one. If we give up on the journey and refuse to follow God, we will have to be rerouted in our race. The end of one race always starts the beginning of the next. Crossing each finish line takes a step of faith. We will never cross the finish line before we're ready to start a new race. We may know the task of the next race, but there will still be a lot of unknowns ahead.

When I was wrapping up my tenure as pastor in Seiling, Oklahoma, God wanted me to take a stand for what was right, which could have meant I had to leave the church. It would have been easier to give in and just go with the current. This situation was complicated and there were a lot of unknowns. Taking a stand might have meant hurting people in the church and my own family, which I was afraid to do.

It is hard when you have the responsibility to make sure your family is taken care of, not with just material things, but make them feel safe and protected. It is also hard when you must uproot your family and move them away from what they're used to. Change is difficult. God was very clear that this was a part of my finish line and whatever happened, it would be okay because God was with me.

When you take a step of faith at the finish line, God's power will show up in a mighty way. I wish I could say that nobody got their feelings hurt. My wife and I were forced to leave the church with the unknown of my next job or where we would live. My children had to leave their school and friends, which was very confusing to them. There was a piece of land my father gave me when he had passed away. I had been trying to sell it for a year with no offers. Within less than a month, God provided the finances we needed to start the next race through the sale of that property.

When we left the church, we moved back to our hometown where we were raised. A pastor friend of mine, whom I had worked for five years, allowed us to move into a trailer on the church property until a church opened up. I asked God to allow us to start pastoring a church and know where we were going to live by the middle of July. We knew school was starting up in August and didn't want any confusion for our kids about where they were going to go to school. It's hard when you don't know the answers your family needs to know, which causes them to feel unsafe and insecure. These things are sometimes harder than financial problems.

I had a church reach out to me at the beginning of July about an interview to become their next pastor. After meeting with the board on a Saturday, they asked me if it was okay if they voted on me becoming their pastor the next day. That happened to be July 15. God honored my prayer for my family and provided confirmation to my wife and I that this was our next race.

God has a way of showing us that we are not alone at any point. We can go through anything and come out of every battle victorious if God is standing with us. As Joshua was crossing his finish line, God was planning his next race.

> *"Now when Joshua was near Jericho, he looked up and saw a man standing in front of him with a drawn sword in his hand. Joshua went up to him and asked, 'Are you for us or for our enemies?' 'Neither,' he replied, 'but as commander of the army of the LORD, I have now come.' Then Joshua fell facedown to the ground in reverence, and asked him, 'What message does my Lord have for his servant?' The commander of the LORD's army replied, 'Take off your sandals, for the place where you are staying is holy.' And Joshua did so." Joshua 5:13-15*

OBEYING GOD

God demonstrated to Joshua that he was not alone and that the Lord would fight his battles. When the angel told him to take off his sandals for this place where he was standing was holy ground, he was referring to the fact that God was with him and was present. God did not want the Israelites to think they were going to destroy their enemies by their own power. He wasn't going to use man's weapons or strategies. When God asks us to do something big and we do not have the power to accomplish it, we trust in the One who gives the promise. God had a plan on how to destroy Jericho and gave it to Joshua:

> *"Then the LORD said to Joshua, 'See, I have delivered Jericho into your hands, along with its king and its fighting men. March around the city once with all the armed men. Do this for six days. Have seven priests carry trumpets of rams' horns in front of the ark. On the seventh day, march around the city seven times, with the priests blowing the trumpets. When you hear them sound a long blast on the trumpets, have the whole army give a loud shout; then the wall of the city will collapse and the army will go up, everyone straight in.'" Joshua 6:2-5*

The gates of Jericho were securely barred due to the presence of the Israelites. No one went out, and no one came in. Any successful passage would be an impossible situation without God. Their weapons could not penetrate Jericho's walls because they were very wide and tall. Rahab, the prostitute, lived within these walls, her window high above—a strategic design to safeguard against potential adversaries.

As long as the gates were shut, nobody could get into Jericho. Yet God told Joshua that He had delivered Jericho into his hands, along with its king and its warriors. Most people couldn't see it the way God did because it would take divine intervention to destroy the wall. God used the Ark of the Covenant, the priest, and their trumpets along with the entire army who began to shout to bring down the wall.

When we do it God's way, with His instructions, it must be precisely what God has told us to do. It wasn't the priest and their trumpets. It wasn't the army of Israel walking around the walls. It wasn't even the shout of the soldiers; it was when they obeyed God that the walls collapsed.

When I prayed for my friend who had cancer, it wasn't my prayer or my own power. Rather, it was the unwavering faith we had in God that He could do anything. And He showed up! God is always faithful to His promises. When God had Jericho's walls collapse, He made sure that the part of the wall Rahab lived in did not collapse; thus, Rahab and all her family were saved.

God is always precise in what He does. If we listen to His plans, we will not go wrong. When the army of the Israelites shouted, the walls came down. I think about how Rahab must have felt when she noticed the walls were shaking. The power of God was demonstrated to her and her family. All the inhabitants of Jericho, including their king and all their fighting men, were killed that day except Rahab and her entire family.

CHAPTER 4

THE RIGHT ALIGNMENT WILL BRING THE RIGHT ASSIGNMENT

Many people embark on life's journey with a promising start, often fueled by a vision or dream from God. However, if we don't align ourselves with the right people, we can be led astray. When we start to pursue God's plan, people who are not in the right alignment with God will lead us off course. I have seen many young people start out with God's plan in place, but because of the people they associate with, they lose focus on the plan God has for them.

GOD HAS A PLAN FOR YOU

In the book of Genesis in the Bible, we see a story about a man named Joseph. As Joseph begins to grow up, God lays out the impact Joseph will have on his family, despite him being one of the youngest in his family. Back in those days, the youngest children really didn't have many opportunities to make an impact. They were often considered the least in the family. For Joseph, God begins to reveal His plan to him through dreams. At the time, Joseph was likely not aware of what those dreams would mean for his life and the future of his family. Here is Joseph sharing his dreams with his older brothers:

> *"He said to them, 'Listen to this dream I had: We were binding sheaves of grain out in the field when suddenly my sheaf rose and stood upright, while your sheaves gathered around mine and bowed down to it.'"*
> *Genesis 37:6-7*

> *"...I had another dream, and this time the sun and moon and eleven stars were bowing down to me."*
> *Genesis 37:9*

Joseph's brothers were jealous of him, but his father kept this matter in mind. Joseph's alignment with his father was what gave him the assignment from God. God will bring people into your life and see something in you. Jacob saw something special in Joseph and knew God had a great purpose for him.

MY WIFE

God will also bring people into your life who will help you and believe in you. Marrying the right person has always been the most important decision in my life. With what God has shared with me about my future, I knew I had to have someone who had a similar calling.

When you are running after God, anyone you align with must be going the same direction. The whole world can be running in a different direction, but to stay on course yourself, the people close to you must head where you are headed, or they will sidetrack you and cause you to trip up.

God has used my wife, Shalene, to confirm the promises He has given me. She reminds me of the promises God has given her about our future. In the Bible, we see the story of Job and all the suffering he experienced. Job was serious about keeping his heart right toward God during the whole thing. However, Job's wife told him to curse God and die. She was not in the right alignment with God and the plan Job had. She could have derailed Job had he not been so focused.

You must have people who understand the plan God has and are hanging on to the promise. There will be times when the promise doesn't look like it will come to pass, or it will feel too difficult to keep going. The people who are in alignment with God will not only encourage you to not quit but also keep seeking the Lord.

HEARING GOD'S PLAN

As we delve deeper into Joseph's story, we uncover how the jealousy of his brothers caused them to throw him into a cistern and subsequently sell him into slavery. Despite the immense difficulty of these trials, God used all of this to position Joseph as second-in-command in Egypt, which brings us back to the two dreams Joseph had about his family bowing down before him in honor.

Although these dreams seemed to initially cause trouble for Joseph, God ultimately used his gift of dream interpretation when it was most needed—during his time in prison. Joseph's interpretation of two fellow inmates' dreams came true and eventually led to his release from prison.

God often doesn't reveal the full blueprint of what we are destined to accomplish. In Joseph's case, God didn't lay out the full scope of the dreams. He didn't tell him that he would be sold into slavery or that he would be in prison for three years. God offers us just enough insight at the beginning so we can hang onto the promise.

When Joseph was cast into the cistern, facing near death, I believe he held onto the promise. When he was sold into slavery, enduring a journey to Egypt, he remembered the promise. And during his three years of imprisonment, when he may have felt forgotten, I believe he held steadfast to the promise. God's plan for my life was revealed through His voice and prophecies He shared through others.

When life throws unexpected curveballs or blindsides me with problems, I have remembered the promise God has given me. It has guided me through some very difficult times. Even though some will never understand my journey ordained by God, suggesting I leave the church I pastor or start over fresh, I've remained committed to the promise God has entrusted me with.

From my perspective, giving up on the promise is giving up on God. God does not make mistakes. Even though I have made lots of mistakes, God has not given up on me. He's not looking for perfection, but a willing vessel to carry out His plan.

WALKING IN GOD'S PLAN

In the initial stages of God's plan, He provides the main objective but doesn't reveal every detail. Consider the case of Moses leaving Egypt. God informed Moses that He was leading the Israelites to a land flowing with milk and honey, the Promised Land. However, God didn't mention He was taking them to the Red Sea, where they would be cornered by the Egyptian army.

Through my own journey, I've come to understand that trusting in God often involves taking one step at a time. God led me to my own Red Sea experiences—challenges that seemed difficult at the time. Yet, as I placed my faith in God, I gradually realized His plans encompassed more than just my personal circumstances. There was a bigger picture at play, and God wanted me to fulfill it.

During my youth, I knew I was called to travel the world as an evangelist. But in my late twenties, God directed me to pastor a church in a small town. This unexpected turn didn't fit my perception of His plan. After three years of pastoring, I came to realize that God had a significant purpose for this church. While I initially viewed it as unrelated to my idea of my future ministry, it actually served as a period of growth and maturity as I was getting started.

Although I wished the church had embraced the vision I shared, I recognized that my role was simply to present the vision and carry out what God had assigned me to do—fulfilling my part in the process. My time at that church was filled with wonderful memories. Yet, as I reflect, I recognize how God used this as a metaphorical Red Sea experience.

As I conveyed the vision to the congregation, certain individuals opposed it, focusing on financial concerns for the church rather than acknowledging the potential positive impact on the town's community. I emphasized that this vision was inspired by God and not men. When the time came for me to leave that church, God miraculously "parted the sea" and opened new doors, signaling an end to that specific phase of the journey and affirming that God was indeed leading me forward.

GOD SHARED HIS PLAN THROUGH OTHERS

God has utilized prophecy as a powerful means to communicate His plans and purpose for my life. It's an incredibly impactful experience when people, unaware of my circumstances, share prophecies about God's future plans. These words serve as a reminder that God has been actively watching over my life, even when I might have felt alone or uncertain.

In 2013, during a night's sleep, a remarkable incident occurred. My wife woke up and observed an angel standing beside my side of the bed. This angel, about five foot and ten inches tall with short hair, held a notepad and was jotting down notes as he looked over me. Upon noticing her presence, he looked briefly at her before returning his attention to me. She closed her eyes, hoping not to be detected, and when she opened them again, he had vanished. This incident provided me assurance when I felt very alone that God was actively involved in every detail of my life.

God doesn't continually repeat His promises when we are impatient or are in the challenges of waiting. There are even moments of silence during the journey. In such instances, there might be a desire for confirmation, especially when doubt creeps in regarding God's timing. God has always given me peace, and it is sufficient even when He chooses to remain silent.

In moments of uncertainty, when questions arise about the journey or timing, God often sends individuals to reinforce His promises. This helps me get rid of the fear that I've taken a wrong turn. God is a good Father and faithful guide who will get us to our promised land.

IN YOUR ASSIGNMENTS

God wants us to be used as a vessel to impact others' lives. This can be through practical assistance or offering financial aid to those in need. My experiences have taught me that anyone can be an instrument of God's grace. Part of that experience is through boldness in sharing prophecies and ministering to others during their times of distress.

To have faith for a miracle, sign, or wonder, spiritual help is often needed. When someone is contemplating killing themselves, material possessions or even encouraging words alone may not suffice. The power of prayer is immense, and through Jesus Christ, we possess the authority to speak life into seemingly dire circumstances. A prophetic word isn't merely about physical presence; it's about being a spiritual force that imparts meaningful change. Through Jesus, we have authority to call those things that are not as though they are (Romans 4:17).

This journey of faith entails a progression from being recipients of grace to becoming channels through which God's power flows. Reflecting on the disciples' relationship with Jesus, we see a pattern of mentorship that equipped them with spiritual gifts to impact lives powerfully. Just as Jesus poured into their lives, when God begins to trust us, He will give us more spiritual gifts to change people's lives. The Bible warns us to not "have a form of godliness but denying its power" (2 Timothy 3:5).

Absolutely, the world needs the power of the Spirit to bring about real transformation. I've come across a lot of hurting people, some rich and some poor, and I've found that true happiness and purpose aren't dependent on material possessions, such as the car you drive or how much money is in your account. People are looking for happiness and purpose in their lives. When we use the spiritual gifts we possess, our assignment can have a much more significant impact in changing lives.

Trust is a crucial aspect, not only in our relationship with God but also in how God entrusts us with His plans and resources. Trust is earned over time, and it's often demonstrated through our faithfulness in smaller tasks. Most people try to make this more complicated than it is. God places situations and opportunities in our lives to gauge our stewardship. When we respond by sharing what we have, helping others, and using our resources wisely, God sees this and entrusts us with even greater responsibilities.

A parable from the Bible about the talents illustrates this concept. The master entrusted different amounts of talents to his servants. The ones who multiplied the talents they were given were rewarded, while the one who buried his talent out of fear and distrust faced harsh consequences. This parable teaches us the principle that those who are faithful with little will be entrusted with more. God desires to bless us and see us multiply the resources He's given us, both materially and spiritually, as we steward them well.

Joseph's story further exemplifies the importance of trusting God's plans even in challenging circumstances. His brothers' jealousy led them to plot against him, and their initial intention was to kill him.

"'Here comes that dreamer!' they said to each other. 'Come now, let's kill him and throw him into one of these cisterns and say that a ferocious animal devoured him. Then we'll see what comes of his dreams.'"
Genesis 37:19-20

The story could have ended there about Joseph, but when God has a plan, man's plans will not succeed. Reuben caught wind of what his brothers were plotting to do to Joseph, and he tried to rescue him. He convinced his brothers to not take his life and not shed any blood. He suggested they throw him into the cistern there in the wilderness but don't lay a hand on him. Reuben's plan was to later rescue him and take him back to his father.

As his brothers sat down to eat their lunch they looked up and saw a caravan of Ishmaelites coming from Gilead. Judah, one of his brothers, said, "What will we gain if we kill our brother? Come, let's sell him to these caravans." What Satan means for bad God can turn around for the good (Genesis 37:26-27a).

When we try to make the right alignments to move us forward on our journey, we will also need to trust God to lead us on this journey. Even though Joshua was taken away from his father, which was his right alignment, Jacob had prepared Joseph and believed he would do great things. People will come along on your journey and try to mess up your purpose in life. God will use their evil plan to bring about His perfect will to save many.

CHAPTER 5

MOVING OUT DAY

LIVING A SUCCESSFUL LIFE

How we define and perceive success will greatly determine our belief in what we are doing. When God is trying to get our attention, He sometimes does it by asking questions. One day, while I was praying, God asked me a question—"Are you successful?"

When God asks me questions, I have learned to pause before I respond and spend much time in prayer waiting for Him to give me an answer. I felt that He wanted me to say yes, but the first response in my heart was no. So, as I sat there, I said to God, "Well, I don't have very much money in the bank. There's not a lot of people going to our church. I'm behind on some bills that I need to pay, and life seems very hard."

This was my way of responding to God without saying no. God was very quiet with no response. A few days later, God began to ask me more questions, but this time, they were direct and to the point. "Are you a good husband? Are you a good father? Do you always try to do what is right? Do you try your best in everything you do?"

Throughout the Word of God, we see Jesus answer a question with a question. God was trying to get something in my heart about how He wanted me to perceive my life. When God asked me the initial question, I first based it off what I had accomplished and how much money I made in a year.

God wanted me to look at my life in a different way than I was perceiving it. What He began to put in my heart was, *You are successful in your life through what money cannot buy.* Money cannot buy me a good marriage. Money cannot make me a better father. Money cannot cause me to make the right decisions. Money can't buy effort. This notion is the foundation of a very successful person.

We cannot control the outcomes that we will experience in life. If we base our success on what we cannot control, we will never feel fulfilled. As God asked me these questions, I began to look at my life in a different way. I am successful by what I can control. I can control the person I am by the decisions I make. I can control putting my best foot forward and working very hard. I can develop good fruit in my life by being connected to Jesus Christ.

> *"I am the vine; you are the branches. If you remain in me and I and you, you will bear much fruit; apart from me you can do nothing." John 15:5*

JOSEPH IN POTIPHAR'S HOUSE

When God gives you a promise, things may go in an opposite direction than you may expect. When you're going against the current, you must hold onto that promise in your heart and keep trusting God in the process.

Having been sold by his brothers, Joseph was now a slave in Egypt. He was bought by Potiphar who was the captain of the Pharoah's guard. Things weren't looking good for Joseph, and he couldn't imagine how this was a part of God's plan. The two dreams he had about his family appeared impossible. He could have easily started feeling sorry for himself, yet Joseph continued to work, and God made him prosperous even as a slave.

On my journey, I have had moments that felt like life wasn't fair, and I would ask God, "Why does this have to happen?" You might be in this place right now. Wondering why God has allowed certain things to happen that seem opposing to His plans. After numerous experiences with this, I know I must be careful to not assume that God has messed up or allowed Satan to bring this trouble. I must trust that God knew this negative was coming, and even though it was unexpected to me, it was not unexpected to God.

As some of your successes stack, people will begin to see the favor of the Lord in your life and either get jealous and talk behind your back or want to partner up with you. Determining people's hearts in this matter is vital to your success. Not everybody will be for you and want you to succeed. Joseph found favor in Potiphar's eyes and was put in charge of his household. He trusted Joseph to care for everything he owned. The Lord began to bless the household of the Egyptian because of Joseph. The blessings of the Lord were on everything Joseph was taking care of for Potiphar including his fields and household.

GOD'S PLAN FOR PROMOTION

Success brings temptation. I'm not talking about the temptation that Joseph had with the offer to sleep with Potiphar's wife. We are not sure that Joseph saw this offer as temptation at all. There is always temptation to go with the flow. If I don't do what my leaders require, even if it is sin, what will my consequence be? These unknowns can cause us to fear doing the right thing even if we're not tempted. These tests are in place to determine our fruit. Jesus said,

> *"A good tree cannot bear bad fruit, and a bad tree cannot bear good fruit." Matthew 7:18*

I can just imagine how Joseph felt at that crossroad. If he slept with Potiphar's wife, he could have kept his job and stayed in

Potiphar's house where God granted him favor and success. If he refused Potiphar's wife, he would lose everything he had worked for and could be killed. God uses these moments to see if we are trustworthy with what He has given us and if we are willing to lose everything we have to do the right thing. God will use struggles, accusations, and lies to get us to the next level.

> *"Now Joseph was well-built and handsome, and after a while his master's wife took notice of Joseph and said, 'Come to bed with me!' But he refused. 'With me in charge,' he told her, 'my master does not concern himself with anything in the house; everything he owns he has entrusted to my care. No one is greater in this house than I am. My master has withheld nothing from me except you, because you are his wife. How then could I do such a wicked thing and sin against God?' And though she spoke to Joseph day after day, he refused to go to bed with her or even be with her. One day, he went into the house to attend to his duties, and none of the household servants was inside. She caught him by his cloak and said, 'Come to bed with me!' But he left his cloak in her hand and ran out of the house. When she saw that he had left his cloak in her hand and had run out of the house, she called her household servants. 'Look,' she said to them, 'this Hebrew has been brought to us to make sport of us! He came in here to sleep with me, but I screamed. When he heard me scream for help, he left his cloak beside me and ran out of the house.'" Genesis 39:6b-15*

Joseph decided to do what was right, and it cost him everything. He was kicked out of the house, fired from his job, and put in prison. Most people would look at this as a demotion, but God set this up as a promotion. It was the necessary step to setting Joseph into Pharaoh's presence. Even though Pharaoh did not yet know anything about Joseph, God was getting Joseph one step closer to His promise.

Joseph faced three great tests in Egypt:

- the test of personal purity—a test that often comes to young people away from home
- the test of opportunity for revenge—a test that often comes to people who have been mistreated
- the test of facing death—a test that often reveals the heart's true position

In each case he overcame the test through his trust in God and His promises.

TESTING YOUR FRUIT

In 2014, my spiritual fruit was tested by God. It was a Wednesday night when I received a phone call from Channel 9 News in Oklahoma City. They said that I was accused of mistreating a renter who was living in a house that I owned. They said that there was no running water or heat in the house. I found out Channel 9 News had already been to the rental house to talk to the family and to hear their accusations. Then they came to my personal house to try to interview me. They took a picture of a rock in my yard that said, "For me and my house, we will serve the Lord."

They were trying to paint a picture of my home and compare it to the rental house. Then they came to the church and pointed out that I was also a pastor. What they failed to mention was the fact that the renter had just moved into the house. When they attempted to have the gas turned on in their name, they were informed that because there had been no gas service to the house for over a year, a pressure test was required first to ensure there were no leaks in the lines before they could turn the gas on. A licensed plumber had to do the work, so we had it scheduled for the next day.

That evening I called Channel 9 News and talked to the news anchor telling him the story. He told me it would be on the ten o'clock news, no matter what the truth was about the situation. He wanted to meet up so he could get my side of the story. As I sat in my car waiting on the news anchor to get to the church, I began to ask the Lord what I needed to do. The Lord told me to apologize about the situation and say we are working on getting everything fixed by tomorrow. Don't give any excuses, just be apologetic.

When I met with the Channel 9 News' anchor and talked with him before the camera started, he said, "I actually believe that you are sincerely sorry for what's going on, and I will do my best to tell your side." When the camera came on, I did my best to do what God had asked me to do. No excuses and no blame for anybody else. I'm sorry the renters are in this situation, and we are working on getting it fixed.

When you get accused and people are treating you as a criminal, it's hard to not tell the whole story. As I walked back to the church to get ready for service, I had a conversation with God. I said, "God, I don't know why people said what they said about me. They knew we were working on it, and we had planned to get it fixed."

The Lord said, "I did this!"

In confusion, I responded to God, "Why?"

The Lord said, "I was testing your fruit. I needed to squeeze you and see what came out, and I was pleased."

God had to know that I truly did care about the people no matter what the situation was. When I showed up at the house the next day with the plumber, I asked them why they called the news. She explained it wasn't her, but rather the neighbor next door. The neighbor found out I was a pastor and said she was going to get things fixed by calling the news. I told her I was sorry this was taking longer than it should and it was to be fixed that day.

When the ten o'clock news came on that night, my family and I watched what they said. My children were pretty upset because they heard how the news report was taking about their dad, but at the end of the story, the news anchor said, "If Larry says he's going to do something, you can count on it."

The next evening, I called the News Channel 9 anchor and told him that we got it fixed and everything was working. He told me the story had already run, and he was not worried about it. I answered, "You said at the end of your newscast that when Larry says something, you can count on it. I wanted you to know I honored my word, and I appreciate what you said."

> *"I am the true vine, and my Father is the gardener. He cuts off every branch in me that bears no fruit, while every branch that does bear fruit he prunes so that it will be even more fruitful. You are already clean because of the word I have spoken to you. Remain in me, as I also remain in you. No branch can bear fruit by itself; it must remain in the vine. Neither can you bear fruit unless you remain in me." John 15:1-4*

God is trying to get His fruit into our lives. Having a spiritually fruitful life isn't just about being a good person or making good choices. It's about letting go of our own desires and living by the Spirit. When you give God control of your life, by letting Him dream through you and plan out your life, you can begin to walk in new territories and adventure to new places for the kingdom of God.

At the start of 2022, God put upon my heart to pray the prayer of Jabez.

> *"Jabez cried out to the God of Israel, 'Oh, that you would bless me and enlarge my territory! Let your hand be with me, and keep me from harm so that I*

will be free from pain.' And God granted his request."
1 Chronicles 4:10

As I prayed this prayer, God began to open new doors in my life for that year. Even though these doors have been very challenging, I found the four-part prayer changed my life. As I asked the Lord to bless me and enlarge my territories, new things kept popping up for me to accomplish.

On March 1, 2022, at nine o'clock at night, the police department called us. A car had driven through our church! We had to remodel the main area of our church, which took nine months. By the end of March 2022, I had received my real estate license. In May 2022, God put on our hearts to sell a property we owned in Sand Springs, Oklahoma. In August 2022, I found out that the long-time renter in a house I owned had passed away. So we started the remodeling process and prepared to sell. In September 2022, God put it on my heart to write this book.

When you first start praying the prayer of Jabez, you focus a lot on God blessing you and broadening your territory. Amid writing this book, I found the last two parts of that prayer are much more important. "Lord, let your hands be with me and keep me from harm." When you release your plans and turn your life completely over to God while accepting His plans, His hands upon your life will keep you focused on doing good and not harm.

CHAPTER 6

STAYING IN IT

While you're on this journey and you're walking with the promise of God, knowing how to stay in it and not give up is part of the process. We accomplish this by letting go of our plan and control of where the journey will take us. This part of God's promise is the longest and hardest.

When God gives you the layout of what He wants you to do, it is an exciting time. You have a purpose and a plan and you're ready to fulfill it. But "staying in it" is a very lonely place sometimes. For my wife and I, we had each other throughout this process. When one of us was struggling in the waiting, the other would remind them of the importance of not giving up and trusting the process.

The longer you're in your journey, the more time you will have to discover there's no place to go but straight. In the beginning, as we started this journey, God gave us options to go to the right or left. Something may pop up looking like an easier road so it will take discernment and discipline to stick with what God has for you.

LETTING GO OF OUR PLAN

While we were pastoring at Power House Church, another church contacted me about sending my resume in. They were looking for a pastor and another pastor recommended they reach out to me. My wife and I were considering sending them a resume and started praying about God's direction. It was a larger church, a bigger salary, and we were excited about the opportunity.

My wife and I decided we would start testing the waters. We took the several-hour car ride to look at the church, knowing it would be a hard move for our family. Our oldest daughter was a junior in high school. So we weighed all our options as we sought the Lord. We had been pastoring at Power House Church for about seven years at this time, and I was not receiving a salary. I started my own business, called Hutch Rock, which was a sandblasting company, to provide income for my family.

64

THE DREAM

Before we started pastoring Power House Church, we had a friend who had a dream. She called my wife and asked her if we were looking at a church in Moore, Oklahoma. We thought she might have overheard us talk about the church we sent our resume to.

Shalene answered, "Yes, why are you asking?"

Maria said, "I had a dream last night, and I could see the whole state of Oklahoma. There was a ribbon that was flowing from Sapulpa to Seiling, Oklahoma. Then the ribbon went from Seiling back to Sapulpa. Now, I see the ribbon going to Moore. I can see a big bow on Moore. I saw two hands reach out from the sky and pull the bow as if opening a present. When the bow came undone, confetti shot all over the state of Oklahoma."

Maria asked God, "What is this confetti?"

And God said, "Those are souls."

As we were testing the waters of leaving the church, God said, "You're not finished, and I have not completed the promise that I gave you."

Even though a new church with a salary would make me feel safer and more secure in taking care of my family, we continued to trust the promise God told us fifteen years earlier.

Back to Joseph. He is in prison because his master's wife falsely accused him of coming into the house to sleep with her. She said, "As soon as I screamed for help, he left his cloak beside me and ran out of the house." (Genesis 39:12) Joseph had been mistreated and lied about by his brothers and now by Potiphar's wife. When you get mistreated and lies are spread about you, revenge will easily find its way to your heart and mind. God was using this to position Joseph for the right moment to help Pharaoh interpret the dreams God had given him.

THE VISION

When I was pastoring in Seiling, Oklahoma, some of the board members at the church feared certain changes we were making in the church. We had just remodeled the sanctuary, and we were talking about breaking ground to build a multi-purpose building. This was a new concept for our board because the church had been out of debt for many years. Even though they agreed that we needed this change, it was still hard.

One of the board members started a rumor about me misusing the church's funds that was very hurtful. Even though this was my first-time pastoring, I cared for the people very deeply. There were about eight hundred people in the town. I had also become the youth pastor in the town and mayor of Seiling. God was using this to remove me from Seiling. It was very painful to be mistreated by people I really cared about.

I can look back now and see how God used this for growth and development. God would not allow me to quit the church but told me I needed to let them vote on the next step of the church and whether I would be the pastor to lead them. I was voted out of the church by eight people. The Sunday before all of this happened, there were over a hundred people at the Sunday service.

While in my office, God reminded me of something in the Bible. He said, "There were two men in the Bible who were stoned. One was Stephen and the other was Paul. In this church, I have had a lot of Stephens who gave up and quit. They walked away from the vision I put in their heart for this church. Now, I need you to be a Paul, for when they stoned him, they dragged him out of the city. But Paul got back up and walked back into the city."

What God taught me that day was no matter how hard ministry gets, don't leave until He tells you to. All the other ministers who pastored that church were punished for their disobedience of walking away from God's vision and plan for their lives. He could not punish the people because they stayed at the church and did not walk away. When you choose to take a stand and go against the current, it will be painful. I can say that God did not punish me for being voted out, but the people who disobeyed God fell under that punishment.

THE BAKER AND THE CUPBEARER

Joseph was put in the same prison where the king's prisoners were confined. The Lord continued to be with Joseph and granted him favor in the eyes of the prison warden, just as he had favor with Potiphar. So the warden put Joseph in charge of all those held in prison, and he was made responsible for all that was done there.

The warden paid no attention to anything under Joseph's care because the Lord was with Joseph and gave him success in whatever he did. When God's hand is upon you, He will guide you to the right places and the right people, even if it's the worst place, like a prison. God made sure that Joseph was in the part of the prison where Pharaoh's servants who upset the king were held so that he could be connected to the king at the right time.

When we live a life of dedication to God, we find ourselves in places that don't make sense. Like Jonah and the big fish. Jonah disobeyed God and ran from Nineveh, but God provided a big fish to save him from drowning and bring him back to the land. God used the prison to connect Joseph to Pharaoh.

Now, there were two servants, the cupbearer and the baker who had offended their master, the king of Egypt. Pharaoh was angry with them and put them in prison. Pharaoh had put them in custody in the house of the captain of the guard, the same prison where Joseph was confined. Joseph found favor with that captain and assigned them to Joseph's care. They had been imprisoned for a while and the cupbearer and baker both had dreams on the same night, but each dream held a meaning of its own (Genesis 40:1-5).

When Joseph saw that the two men were frustrated one morning, he asked why they were sad:

> "'We both had dreams,' they answered, 'but there is no one to interpret them.' Then Joseph said to them, 'Do not interpretations belong to God? Tell me your dream.' So the chief cupbearer told Joseph his dream.*

He said to him, 'In my dream I saw a vine in front of me, and on the vine were three branches. As soon as it budded, it blossomed, and its clusters ripened into grapes. Pharaoh's cup was in my hand, and I took the grapes, squeezed them into Pharaoh's cup and put the cup in his hand.' 'This is what it means,' Joseph said to him. 'The three branches are three days. Within three days Pharoah will lift up your head and restore you to your position, and you will put Pharaoh's cup in his hand, just as you used to do when you were his cupbearer. But when all goes well with you, remember me and show me kindness; mention me to Pharaoh and get me out of prison.'" Genesis 40:8-14

God gave the cupbearer this dream and used Joseph to interpret the dream. When God gives you a promise, its purpose is for you to rest. God has planned every person's life and every step along the way. God says He judges the heart of every man. When the cupbearer was being punished, God had plans to restore the cupbearer right beside Pharaoh for a divine appointment. The baker also had a dream:

"When the chief baker saw that Joseph had given a favorable interpretation, he said to Joseph, 'I too had a dream: On my head were three baskets of bread. In the top basket were all kinds of baked goods for Pharaoh, but the birds were eating them out of the basket on my head.' 'This is what it means,' Joseph said. 'The three baskets are three days. Within three days Pharaoh will

lift off your head and impale your body on a pole. And the birds will eat away your flesh.'" Genesis 40:16-19

People get confused about the baker's dream because they feel he died unjustly. When God judged his heart, it's my belief that He found the baker with wrongdoing. The baker's dream was not for himself, but for the cupbearer to hear what would happen to the baker.

"Now the third day was Pharaoh's birthday, and he gave a feast for all his officials. He lifted up the heads of the chief cupbearer and the chief baker in the presence of his officials: He restored the chief cupbearer to his position, so that he once again put the cup into Pharaoh's hand—but he impaled the chief baker, just as Joseph had said to them in his interpretation. The chief cupbearer, however, did not remember Joseph; he forgot him." Genesis 40:20-23

I believe the chief cupbearer forgot about Joseph because it wasn't time to reveal his gift. The cupbearer saw his dream come true and he was restored to his position, but he also saw the chief baker's dream come true. Sometimes, when two things happen simultaneously, God will use them to prepare the way and open a door at the right time.

Trust the process and stay in it. What is God looking for from you in the process of staying in it? The right attitude.

GOD LOVES A CHEERFUL GIVER

"Each of you should give what you have decided in your heart to give, not reluctantly or under compulsion, for God loves a cheerful giver." 2 Corinthians 9:7

When you are going through the process and trusting God, having the right attitude is key to God's heart. We are called by God to do hard things, even though we would like life to be easy. As we look throughout the Word of God, we see people doing the impossible. When we give our best to God, we need to do it cheerfully and with thanksgiving.

There are many things we pursue in life, like when I was called to do crusades around America. God specifically warned me not to live for those events but rather enjoy the process, or I would live with regrets. I had this call on my life when my wife and I were married. She was nineteen, and I was twenty years old. We originally planned on waiting to have children, but a little over a year into our marriage, we were pregnant with our first child. I'd never seen my wife happier as she was told she would not be able to have children. We had three girls before we were twenty-five years old. I know now God wanted me to be the best husband and father I could be.

Even though I was doing exactly what God wanted me to do at the time by caring for my family, carrying this call to do crusades for the Lord felt like a constant pressure. I would describe it as hard to breathe as if it was sitting on my chest and in the forefront of my mind. At the age of twenty-five, I really didn't know what was so important about being a good husband and a father. But looking back, I see the impact my presence had on my wife and our children's lives. I now have my best friend standing beside me and believing in the same dream God gave us. I have three daughters who see me as a role model of what a good husband looks like.

I would have missed so much if all I tried to do was focus and prematurely fulfill the plans God gave me. God had a perfect timing for all those plans to come into my life, but I needed to focus on the moment right where I was at for a little while. I had to practice being my best, giving all that I had to God so that it would define me as the person I am today.

ATTITUDE OF YOUR MIND

> *"You were taught, with regard to your former way of life, to put off your old self, which is being corrupted by its deceitful desires; to be made new in the attitude of your mind; and to put on the new self, created to be like God in true righteousness and holiness."*
> *Ephesians 4:22-24*

We are to reflect God's attitude and put off our own because it will corrupt us through our deceitful desires. We cannot change our attitude on our own. We are created in His image, so we must be made new, which will also be a process as we go.

In slavery, Joseph could have had a bad attitude and done a lot of complaining; he had a right to in most people's eyes. Do you have a bad attitude? Joseph continued to look for opportunities to show how great God was by interpreting dreams for Him. The cupbearer didn't forget about Joseph and the interpretations of the dreams. They had left his mind and at that moment when Pharaoh gave back his position, he did not mention Joseph to anybody. God will bring things back to people's minds at the right time, which is exactly what He did for Joseph.

CHAPTER 7

THE UNEXPECTED

After Joseph had given the interpretation to the cupbearer and baker, he remained in prison for two years with no word from the cupbearer. It looked like all hope was lost. Occasionally, he likely thought that prison would be his new home, but he did hold onto hope in the dream he had when he was seventeen. He knew he would see his brothers and father again because of this promise. Hope is a very powerful thing.

When unexpected things happen in life, you must keep hope at the forefront of your mind. If you don't, you'll start on a roller coaster ride. In one moment, you'll be up high, trusting God, and in the next moment, you'll feel so low that you'll lose all hope. Having faith in God doesn't take away the unexpected challenges you'll face in life. We can always trust the Lord and know that He will work things out for good, but unexpected events will test your heart in the process of trust.

Pharaoh was the king of Egypt. He wielded the power to kill anyone he pleased for no good reason. Nobody dared to question him, and everyone lived in fear of him. If he grew dissatisfied with one of his wives, he could order her execution without hesitation. The king didn't need to seek permission from his wives to marry another woman. He had unlimited wealth, a vast entourage of servants, and complete authority. If he found himself unable to sleep at night, he would summon a servant to read him stories or offer wine until he fell unconscious.

However, God disrupted his seemingly perfect life with a dream. Pharaoh recognized that this was an unexpected dream and needed to uncover its meaning, as it was of divine origin. He turned to the magicians and wise men of Egypt, but no one could interpret the dream. Here is the description of the dream:

> "...He was standing by the Nile, when out of the river there came up seven cows, sleek and fat, and they grazed among the reeds. After them, seven other cows, ugly and gaunt, came up out of the Nile and stood beside those on the riverbank. And the cows that were ugly and gaunt ate up the seven sleek, fat cows. Then Pharaoh woke up. He fell asleep again and had a second dream: Seven heads of grain, healthy and good, were growing on a single stalk. After them, seven other heads of grain sprouted—thin and scorched by the east

wind. The thin heads of grain swallowed up the seven healthy, full heads. Then Pharaoh woke up; it had been a dream." Genesis 41:1-7

These two dreams had the same meaning, and Joseph was renowned for his ability to interpret dreams. The cupbearer's recollection of Joseph wasn't due to his success or his position in prison. Often, we assume that we'll be known for our achievements or accomplishments in life. However, it's the gifts bestowed upon us by God that define us. What God has planted in our heart, only we can bring to fruition. While we all have a role to play, the glory ultimately belongs to God.

The cupbearer proceeded to inform Pharaoh about Joseph and how he interpreted the dreams.

"Pharaoh was once angry with his servants, and he imprisoned me and the chief baker in the house of the captain of the guard. Each of us had a dream the same night, and each dream had a meaning of its own. Now the young Hebrew was there with us, a servant of the captain of the guard. We told him our dreams, and he interpreted them for us, giving each man the interpretation of his dream. And things turned out exactly as he interpreted them to us: I was restored to my position, and the other man was impaled." Genesis 41:10-13

This situation with the cupbearer was used by God to position Joseph where he belonged, and the journey equipped Joseph for the opportune moment that would arrive. His gift for dream interpretation elevated him from a prisoner to the second-in-command of Egypt.

THE INTERPRETATION OF THE DREAMS

"Then Joseph said to Pharaoh, 'The dreams of Pharaoh are one and the same. God has revealed to Pharoah what He is about to do. The seven good cows are seven years, and the seven good heads of grain are seven years; it is one and the same dream. The seven lean, ugly cows that came up afterward are seven years, and so are the seven worthless heads of grain scorched by the east wind: they are seven years of famine. It is just as I said to Pharaoh: God has shown Pharaoh what he is about to do. Seven years of great abundance are coming throughout the land of Egypt, but seven years of famine will follow them. Then all the abundance of Egypt will be forgotten, and the famine will ravage the land. The abundance in the land will not be remembered, because the famine that follows it would be so severe. The reason the dream was given to Pharaoh in two forms is that the matter has been firmly decided by God, and God will do it soon. And now let pharaoh look for a discerning and wise man and put him in charge of the land of Egypt. Let pharaoh appoint commissioners over the land to take a fifth of the harvest of Egypt during the seven years of abundance. They should collect all the food of these good years that are coming and store up the

*grain under the authority of Pharaoh, to be kept in
the cities for food. This food should be held in reserve
for the country, to be used during the seven years of
famine that will come upon Egypt, so that the country
may not be ruined by the famine.' The plan seemed
good to Pharaoh and to all his officials. So Pharaoh
asked them, 'Can we find anyone like this man, one in
whom has the spirit of God?'" Genesis 41:25-38*

Joseph's ability to interpret dreams came to the forefront when he
explained Pharaoh's visions, providing insight into the coming
fourteen years. Pharaoh perceived Joseph not through the lens
of his past as a prisoner or slave but as a divine gift and vessel of
the wisdom of God.

While it's natural to hope that the unexpected doesn't occur,
we should lean on the Lord for His wisdom and guidance
when facing the unforeseen. At times, we'll be called upon to
fulfill others' dreams. Even though Pharaoh held authority as
king, he lacked the wisdom to safeguard his people. Joseph,
infused with God's wisdom, stepped in and prepared for the
impending famine.

During a cruise to Mexico with my wife, we had been sailing
for about five days. Our cruise ship docked in La Paz, Mexico,
yet we had planned to remain onboard and unwind. That
morning, I heard the Lord say, "Today will be one of the most
challenging days of your life." Initially, I thought to myself that I
was simply looking forward to a massage, relaxation by the pool,
and enjoying meals on the ship. I didn't dwell too much on the

message; I didn't even mention it to my wife as I perceived it as a personal message from God and something I alone would have to deal with.

We got up and went to breakfast before heading for our scheduled massages. After our massages, I met up with my wife at the waiting area to discuss our plans. She mentioned that she wasn't feeling well and wanted to return to our room to rest. Concerned, I asked if she was okay. She explained that she felt unusually tired after the massage and needed to lie down. Even thought she was not feeling well, we decided to spend some time in the men's and women's steam rooms before heading back to our room. So we went our separate ways—my wife to the women's locker room and I to the men's.

About fifteen minutes later, I exited the men's locker room to check on my wife's readiness to return to our room. A staff member from the spa informed me that she had already returned to our room to rest. Finding her in the room, visibly fatigued and quiet, I let her know that I was going to work out in the gym and would check on her in around forty-five minutes.

When I returned to the room after my workout, she was still asleep. I decided to give her more time to rest and went to have lunch. A couple of hours later, I went back to check on her, and she was still in bed. She told me she had fainted in the bathroom and was not feeling any better. She needed to go to the medical center.

Upon calling the medical center, we were told they were closed and would reopen at 4:00 p.m. By around 3:30 p.m., her pain had intensified to the point she couldn't stand or walk. I immediately called back, emphasizing her emergent condition and requested a wheelchair, as she was unable to walk. Upon reaching the medical center, they started blood work and discovered her blood pressure was extremely low, and she had intense stomach pain.

After approximately thirty minutes, the doctor entered the room and let us know her appendix was about to rupture. He said we needed to get off the ship and get to the nearest hospital. While my wife was very concerned about receiving medical care in Mexico, a brief conversation with the doctor made us realize that we had no choice. As the doctor suggested, I went and packed our bags so we could get off the ship.

There were so many unknowns going through my mind all at once, but what the Lord spoke to my heart that morning came back to my mind about it being one of the hardest days of my life. After packing our bags, I kept getting phone calls from the ship's staff telling me I needed to hurry so they could leave the port and make sure I paid my bills for the cruise and for the medical center. When I got down to the medical center, they had already taken Shalene off the ship, and she was waiting beside an ambulance. They said the bill was over $1,500.00 just for the medical side of things. After paying, they escorted me off the ship.

Shalene was waiting on a stretcher beside the ambulance. When I got to her, a worker from the cruise ship said he needed our passports and would talk to us tomorrow at the hospital. I handed our two passports to the gentleman, and we got into the ambulance and started on our way to the hospital.

As I was sitting in the front seat of the ambulance, I began to talk to God about all of this. My first question to the Lord was, "If you knew this was going to happen and you warned me this morning, why didn't you stop this from happening?" The Lord was very quiet, and He didn't give me an answer, but I could feel Him very close to me on the way to the hospital. I knew I would need to make a payment when I got to the hospital, so I started moving money around in different accounts so I would be ready to make that payment.

When we got to the hospital and unloaded our luggage in the emergency room, they began to evaluate Shalene and perform an ultrasound on her appendix. They ruled out her appendix, and her blood work was normal. By this time, it was 9:00 p.m., and the cruise ship was on its way to Loreto, Mexico. We told the doctor we couldn't be released because we had no passports, and we did not know how we were going to find a place to stay tonight.

The worker from the cruise showed up at the hospital and told them we needed to stay the night and get a doctor's report the next morning. If Shalene was healthy enough to get back on the ship, they would require a doctor's note. We knew that the ship would be at the next port on the next day in Loreto. If everything went well through the night, we would have to figure out how we were going to get to Loreto and back on the ship.

The next morning, the doctor came in and gave us a good report. The worker from the ship said we would have to go by car and pay a driver for the four-hour drive. I took all our luggage out to the front of the hospital while waiting for the driver as the hospital staff wheeled my wife out in a wheelchair. When I checked to see how far away our driver was, I noticed that the driver was named Jesus. I turned to my wife and said, "Jesus is coming to pick us up and get us back on the ship!" We arrived just in time to rejoin our ship.

Those twenty-four hours were very unexpected and turbulent. But we both leaned on the Lord for His protection. As I reflected on the warning from the Lord that morning, I'm glad He didn't tell me what was going to happen. But His peace throughout that process made it a better situation. I knew everything was going to be okay. No matter what happened, God was with us.

The unexpected will happen in your life, but you are not alone. Pharaoh was not expecting to have a life-changing dream. But God placed the answer to the dream right beside him without him even knowing it.

CHAPTER 8

DON'T LEAVE THE BOAT

STORMS WILL COME

In the book of Acts, we see Paul sailing in a boat, making slow headway for many days, and having difficulty arriving off Cnidus. When the wind did not allow them to hold their course, they sailed to the isle of Crete, opposite Salmone. They moved along the coast with difficulty and came to a place called Fair Havens, near the town of Lasea.

Like Paul, the current will sometimes cause the process to move slowly or take you off course from where you originally thought you should go. Sometimes the current can turn into a powerful storm. Storms are hard to explain when it comes to following

God because they often will come suddenly. At first, the winds might help you along on the journey, but they can also turn into a hurricane before you know it. We have trials that seem impossible, and while God allows those trials to come in full force, don't leave the boat. God has placed you in a specific time and place. He will not leave you when the storm comes because it's a part of the process.

On May 19, 2013, at our Sunday morning service, God told me there was a devastation coming to Moore, Oklahoma, and that we needed to be ready and pray for people's safety. The news channel issued a warning stating everyone needed to be underground when this tornado came through Moore, Oklahoma. I had been on a nine-day water-only fast and my plans were to fast for forty days. After the service, God said I needed to go off my fast and be ready to help. I asked the Lord if He could keep this tornado from happening. His answer was, "No."

Monday, May 20th, was a very unusual day for me. I had a flat tire on the highway and had to have my vehicle towed to a tire shop. My wife came and picked me up because we knew the storm was coming that evening and we needed to be ready. My wife continued to tell me that we needed to be underground because of how big this tornado was going to be. We arrived at a title company that had a basement. I didn't know the people at the title company but later learned that they had been praying for a minister to come to the title company for shelter.

When we arrived at the title company, we could see the tornado headed in our direction. There were about fifty people in the basement. I'm not sure why I was not scared or even nervous. I believe it was because I had been fasting, and I knew God was with us. My father-in-law stood up and asked if I could pray so everybody could feel calm.

As I started to pray, we could hear the tornado going over the top of our building. I began to pray louder so the people could hear my prayer instead of the loud noise of the tornado. After about forty-five seconds, the tornado passed by. A gentleman and I wanted to get out of the building to survey the damage and see if it was safe for everybody to leave the basement. When I stepped outside, I could not get my bearings because most of the buildings around us had collapsed and most of the vehicles were gone. Several people ran over to help, and together, we found some tools to open the door to the basement where all our family was taking cover.

The amazing thing was the tornado had gone around us instead of directly hitting our building. All the cars were gone in the parking lot, except the ones that were near the title company. The tornado removed the roof of the building, but the walls were still standing. When you are in a storm, God will be with you, so you do not have to fear.

Paul's ship was caught by the storm and could not head into the wind, so rather than fighting it, he gave way to keep the ship together while he and the rest of the crew were driven along. Then they passed rope under the ship to hold it together. I don't

know about you, but I don't want my promise from God to be
held together by a rope. But there may be times it feels like it
can all fall apart at any moment.

Paul's boat took such a violent battering from the storm that the
next day they began to throw the cargo overboard (Acts 27:15).
I can imagine for those who didn't know God or trust Him that
this created a sense of desperation and concern for how they
would manage without those precious and necessary provisions.
There may be times when you will feel that all is lost. At various
moments on my journey, I prepared to explain why I fell short
of God's promise and was about ready to quit because I didn't
see any other way. At the precise right moment, God would
come through. His faithfulness is without measure (Acts 27:20).

AN ANGEL APPEARED TO PAUL

> *"Last night an angel of the God to whom I belong
> and whom I serve stood beside me and said, 'Do not
> be afraid, Paul. You must stand trial before Caesar;
> and God has graciously given you the lives of all who
> sail with you.' So keep up courage, men, for I have
> faith in God that it will happen just as he told me."*
> *Acts 27:23-25*

God was reminding Paul that He was with him on this journey,
and the storm was a part of the process. He was guiding the
ship to its perfect destination. God's plan was to have him stand
before Caesar and tell him about Jesus. That boat carrying Paul
looked like it was on its last leg and going to sink. I have felt like

DON'T LEAVE THE BOAT

that sometimes with the promises that God has given me. I've said to God, "Why do you want to use this church? Can we not just get a different church?"

God doesn't see things the way we do. He doesn't look at the size of the tree, He looks at the size of the fruit. God was looking at Paul's fruit, not at the broken-down boat. As Paul was asleep, an angel came and stood beside him and revealed the bigger picture—that he would stand before Caesar.

RELEASING THE LIFEBOAT

> *"Then Paul said to the centurion and the soldiers, 'Unless these men stay with the ship, you cannot be saved.' So the soldiers cut the ropes that held the lifeboat and let it drift away." Acts 27:31-32*

Staying in the boat means not looking for another way out. You must release all lifeboats from the promise even if the promise is being held together by rope. God's protection is within the promise and not within your power to control it. God does not have to keep you safe outside the promise. His commitment is within the promise. It doesn't matter what you must overcome whether it's giants, snakes, or armies.

Like the Israelites in the wilderness, God promised that their children would return to the Promised Land, so He had to keep them safe. He gave them manna and quail to eat, and He gave them water out of a rock. Throughout the forty years of wandering, their clothes and shoes did not wear out. When you stay in the promise, you will have God with you and His hand on your life.

In ministry, anytime I have lifeboats attached, they are more of a distraction. I find myself continually asking God, "Is it time to get out of the boat? Is there a new way You want me to go?" or I just say, "I don't think this boat is going to make it." When you release the lifeboats from the promise, your total faith is in the process. You're no longer looking for a way out of the promise, but you're continuing the conversation with God about what is next on this journey.

There is a misconception that when things are not going well, it's time to abandon the ship. Let me give you an example of trusting the process and keeping faith and what God has said. God promised Abraham that he would be father to the nations. He promised him a son of his own flesh and blood who would be his heir.

> *"He took Abraham outside and said, 'Look up at the sky and count the stars— if indeed you can count them.' Then he said to him, 'So shall your offspring be.'" Genesis 15:5*

He took him outside his tent and said, "Look at the sand, if you indeed can count them." Then he said to him again, "So shall your offspring be." The promise God was making to a then childless Abraham was that his future descendants would be too numerous to count. Later, God gave Abraham a son and fulfilled His promise.

God decided we cannot have any lifeboats. So one morning, He told Abraham to go sacrifice his only son to the Lord, which is totally against God's nature. Trusting God, Abraham knew even if he sacrificed his son, God could raise him from the dead. Abraham removed all the lifeboats and trusted completely in God.

Abraham and his son, Isaac, were headed to the mountain to worship God and make a sacrifice. Isaac did not understand where the animal they were to sacrifice was. So he asked Abraham about it. Abraham responded, "God will provide." He trusted the process, and God indeed provided, while first, making sure Abraham was completely leaning on Him. For God said:

> "...Now I know that you fear God, because you have not withheld from me your son, your only son."
> Genesis 22:12

LANDING IN THE RIGHT SPOT

On this journey, you will feel at times like you are not in control and are just being dragged along by the storm. But remember, God is in control of the storm, and He will use them to get you to your destination. Anytime you take a step of faith, there will be opposition as part of the process. The key is to keep your eyes on Jesus, not the storms. When we put our trust in God, He will have us do things that will impact His kingdom. If we look at the storms, fear will come into our hearts. But when we look at Jesus through the storm, the destination will be the plan of Jesus and nothing will stop us.

When the people on the boat were safely on shore, they found out that they were on the island of Malta. That was not their original destination, but it's where the storm brought them. It was rainy and cold, and the islanders showed unusual kindness, built a fire, and welcomed them all. As Paul was gathering a pile of brushwood to put on the fire, a viper, driven out by the heat of the fire, bit him on the hand. When the islanders saw the snake hanging from Paul's hand, they said to each other:

> *"... This man must be a murderer; for though escaped from the sea, the goddess of Justice has not allowed him to live." Acts 28:4*

People will always have an opinion about you based off anything and everything, including your accomplishments and defeats. If you accomplish something great, they will be jealous of you or think you must have cheated to get there. Like in Paul's situation, the islanders assumed he must have been a murderer because of a snake bite.

> *"But Paul shook the snake off into the fire and suffered no ill effects. The people expected him to swell up or suddenly fall dead; but after waiting a long time and seeing nothing unusual happened to him, they changed their minds and said he was a god." Acts 28:5-6*

Their opinion about Paul changed just as quickly when they saw nothing come of the bite. On this journey, there will be opportunities to make an impact for the kingdom of God. I have learned that this has little to nothing to do with God's people, but He allows things to happen along the way because of His compassion for the lost. When we look through God's perspective, the storm directed them to this island because God cared for those people.

The islanders might not have understood Paul's situation, but they knew something about him was pretty amazing. Because of this miracle, the people listened to Paul and brought the sick to him so they could be healed.

> *"There was an estate nearby that belonged to Publius, the chief official of the island. He welcomed us to his home and showed us generosity hospitality for three days. His father was sick in bed, suffering from fever and dysentery. Paul went to him and, after prayer, placed hands on him and healed him. When this had happened, the rest of the sick on the island came and were cured. They honored us in many ways; and when we were ready to sail, they furnished us with supplies we needed." Acts 28:7-10*

God always has a plan on how to get you to your destination. For Paul and his shipmates, all seemed lost; they had no food, water, or transportation. The storm took everything they had, but Paul still had the mission God gave him. Paul never asked for one thing and was able to be a blessing to the people of Malta, allowing them to experience the power of God. Their hearts were changed, and they furnished Paul and the others with all the supplies they needed.

CHAPTER 9

DO IT GOD'S WAY

When we look back at these stories of Abraham, Moses, Joseph, and Paul, we can see doing it God's way is the only way the corresponding promises will come about. What do I mean when I use the phrase, doing it God's way?

> *"Whoever does not love does not know God, because God is love." 1 John 4:8*

When we do things for God, it must be out of love. Let's look at giving to God. If you're giving just to get something from God that is not an expression of love. If you're giving to God because you appreciate Him that is an expression of your love. But if we are giving to help someone out, because God has asked us to, this is an expression of our love toward God.

"Suppose a brother or a sister is without clothes or daily food. If one of you says to them, 'Go in peace; keep warm and well fed,' but does nothing about their physical needs, what good is it?" James 2:15-16

GOD'S LOVE

Moses's mission was to liberate the people from slavery, but he initially attempted to achieve this through his own means. Observing an Egyptian soldier mistreating an Israelite, Moses took matters into his own hands and killed the soldier. However, this plan was not God's way, but you can still see the expression of love for the people.

God's objective was not to inflict harm upon the Egyptians; instead, it aimed to free His people from Egypt and lead them back to the land He had promised to Jacob. Due to Pharaoh's stubbornness, this process eventually led to Egypt's downfall. God was well aware that it would necessitate all ten plagues to compel Ramses, the king of Egypt, to release the Israelites.

Moses' reluctance to return to Egypt to free the Israelites, displeased God, as it lacked evident love for His people. Moses had previously attempted his own way, which had failed. However, God was now guiding him back to Egypt, illustrating the importance of following God's way through love and obedience. By complying, Moses would be expressing his love for God and His people.

God's love was deeper than merely setting the Israelites free. He sought to honor His promise to Jacob and guide the people back to the bountiful land promised to Abraham and his descendants—a land flowing with milk and honey. This love also encompassed future generations.

Even Egypt did not escape God's love. He granted Pharaoh a dream, foreshadowing seven years of prosperity followed by seven years of famine. This dream served to not only save Pharaoh and Egypt but also safeguard Jacob's family and their legacy. Joseph's journey, orchestrated by God, positioned him beside Pharaoh due to his exceptional ability to interpret dreams, and many lives were spared, which was a profound manifestation of God's love.

As we embrace God's way, we have our part to do, and God will perform the miracles. Fulfilling God's promises involves showing up at the right time and place. God harnessed Joseph's brothers' jealousy to redirect his path.

God's love was seen through Him saving Moses from being killed as a child. He used the faith of Moses' mother to put Moses on the right path. God used the rebellion of the people to send Moses away from Egypt so he could find the mountain of God. He used the miracle at the mountain to speak to Moses through a burning bush at the right time.

In the story of Paul, we see the love of God used the religious people to put Paul in prison and put him on the right path to go before Caesar. God used the storm to reroute them to the island of Malta and the snake to show His power to the people, so they could know the healing power of God. God's plan for you is to do it His way. This might mean you'll have to go through storms and difficult times, but you will arrive at the destination God wants you to be at.

THE EXPRESSION OF LOVE

> *"Love is patient, love is kind. It does not envy, it does not boast, it is not proud. It does not dishonor others, it is not self-seeking, it is not easily angered, it keeps no record of wrongs. Love does not delight in evil but rejoices with the truth. It always protects, always trusts, always hopes, always perseveres." 1 Corinthians 13:4-7*

When we choose to do it God's way, we will have expressions of love going to others. Sometimes, in our day-to-day life with family and doing business with others, it is hard to continually express love in these ways. It is important to examine the way we treat others and what that says about our hearts. Here are some questions from 1 Corinthians 13 we can ask ourselves and consistently find areas we can improve in.

EXAMINING OUR HEART

Am I patient?

We must determine to have patience behind our actions and behaviors in how we treat others. Love as patience here is characterized by God the Father, Son, and Holy Spirit. We must seek to grow in this kind of love.

Do I live to love others, or am I self-seeking?

We must investigate our hearts and again, check our motives. This does not mean we shouldn't want to be successful, but it's a determination in our hearts for why we want to be successful. For example, in self-motivation, we might be doing something to have nicer things. Of course, you must set goals to accomplish things that you want, but be sure to also set goals for what you want to do for others as God makes you successful.

Do I delight in evil, or do I rejoice with truth?

This is a harder question. Truth does not change. It's not an opinion or a belief. The truth is a statement from God in His Word. For example, "God does not lie," or "God is good." These statements do not change and are truth. When we rejoice in truth, we are stating that truth lives in us. There are many discussions about what is written in the Bible and what people believe. When you believe in the truth of God's Word, you do not argue or try to figure out a different way to believe what you want to. You accept the truth. When you accept the truth, it will change you. Your belief should not be formed from a person or church but through the truth of God's Word.

DON'T BE EASILY ANGERED

One guarantee we all have is that people will hurt our feelings and do us wrong. When this happens, we can show love by not being easily angered, which we cannot do in our own strength. God has given me a tool to help me not to get easily angered.

When I give people the benefit of the doubt, it allows me to look at it from their perspective, rather than the hurt that I feel. We have not all been raised the same way or taught the same compassion toward others.

In my early twenties, I was managing some apartments my family owned. A lady was renting a one-bedroom apartment, and she decided to move out because she didn't have enough money for rent. So I called her about her things and getting the key from her. She said she had no way to get her things out because she didn't have a truck, so I arranged to take her stuff to where she was moving.

When I showed up to the apartment, her brother said that he was going to move into her apartment, and if I wanted him to get him out, I would have to take him to court and evict him. I told him I had already talked to his sister, and I was taking her stuff to her new place and that he would have to find a new place to live. I added that I could give him a ride somewhere, but he could not stay there because we did not have a lease with him.

After giving him a ride to his cousin's house, I went back to the apartment to load up my truck. After filling it with her things and tying them down securely, I saw four people running down the street toward me screaming they were going to kill me for taking their things. My first response was to run into the apartment and try to lock the door, but my truck door was open, and I didn't want to give them access to my vehicle. So I started walking toward them and tried to calm them down.

One of the men was the renter's brother whom I had given a ride to earlier, and the other three men were his cousins. They were coming to beat me up. All four of them were surrounding me and pushing me. They said I was not going to take that stuff anywhere because some of it belonged to the renter's brother. I told him he could take whatever he needed that was his, but that didn't seem to calm him down.

The renter's brother said he wanted to call the police because he thought I was stealing his things. I told him I thought it was a great idea and offered to call them myself. The police showed up and in about ten minutes they started talking to the gentleman to find out what was going on. One of the police officers came over to me to ask me what was happening, and I told him the whole story.

The officer I was talking to asked if these men were trespassing on my property, and I told him they were. So the officer brought me over to the four men and asked me if I wanted these men to be arrested for trespassing. I said, "Not the three cousins, just the renter's brother."

The officer said to the other officer, "Tell him he's under arrest for trespassing."

The officers arrested the renter's brother but let the other three leave as they were likely coerced into coming up there to cause trouble. I told them if they don't come back, they won't be arrested. As I was sitting in the car with the police officer, he said, "I can't believe you're sitting in my car able to give this police report."

I didn't understand what he was saying, so he responded by saying, "I put these three cousins, who you let go, in jail every weekend because of bar fights." As I look back at this story, I can see God's protection, but I've also learned to give people the benefit of the doubt, even when they don't deserve it.

My mom always taught me, "You work to give." I would watch my mom pay for people's food inside restaurants and give a hundred-dollar bill to a mother to help her buy diapers for her baby. She taught me when you find a need, go the extra mile. Giving the benefit of the doubt means you were raised to do what is right but cannot expect everybody to treat you the same.

ALWAYS PROTECTS AND ALWAYS TRUSTS

When we do it God's way, we show Him that we trust His plan is perfect. We know God will show us His plan so others may know His love. His plan will require us to trust Him in the process. In the story of Moses, we see God's love expressed through His deliverance of the Israelites from the slavery. He wasn't coming just to deliver them from Egypt but to protect and defend them from the wickedness that had enslaved them. He was coming to the rescue, not only to show the Egyptians not to mess with God's people again, but also every enemy from that day forward. God showed that He loved the Israelites so much that if anyone were to mess with them, they would know they were messing directly with God.

When Moses trusted how God wanted to deliver the Israelite people, he was trusting Him to bring them out victoriously.

Moses was simply asking the pharaoh to let the Israelite people go so they may worship and sacrifice to their God. Pharaoh not only let them go but had the Egyptian people give them gold and clothing as they left Egypt.

God also gave the Israelites victory by killing all the Egyptian soldiers who were chasing them by causing the Red Sea to come crashing down on them. After the Israelites had crossed the Red Sea and made it onto dry ground, God allowed the waves of the parted sea to sweep the soldiers into the water where they died. They won a great battle that day without any fighting.

ALWAYS HOPES AND ALWAYS PERSEVERES

What does it look like to remain in hope and persevere through the process of the journey with our loving God?

> *"Consider it pure joy, my brothers and sisters, whenever you face trials of many kinds, because you know that the testing of your faith produces perseverance. Let perseverance finish its work so that you may be mature and complete, not lacking anything." James 1:2-4*

The hope that God gives you allows you to persevere so the testing of your faith may produce fruit. The hope in this promise will allow you to persevere, so you may become mature and complete lacking nothing that God wants to teach you in the process of the journey.

> *"Blessed is the one who perseveres under trial because, having stood the test, that person will receive the*

crown of life that the Lord has promised to those who love him." James 1:12

When we are loving God, we will persevere through trials. When we have stood the test, we will receive the crown of life the Lord promised to all His children—those who love Him. To love God is to express hope that we trust Him and persevere through the process because He will finish what He started in our lives.

I have followed God with my whole heart, and though it has been difficult, I would not change it for the world because it has formed who I am and what I believe. We are often called to do difficult things for God, so keep hope alive in your heart so you may persevere through every trial and see God show off in your life. We serve a mighty God!

CONCLUSION

I LOVE YOU, GOD'S WAY

Many years ago, my family and I would argue about who loves each other more. It was the typical, "I love you more." "No, I love you more," back and forth. God's love is the greatest love we can ever experience. So when my children and friend's children are saying goodbye to me, the first one to say, "I love you God's way," would win because I explained we cannot love someone more than God can.

His love is based off the Word of God and not our feelings of being loved. God's love is about the bigger picture, which is the kingdom of God. He will not always choose sides between two people or favor one person over another. Sometimes it will feel unfair when things don't go the way you want life to go. People will become angry at God when they don't understand why bad things happened in their life. We need to know in life, bones will still break, and trials will still come.

Christians must go against the current because of God's immense patience and love for others. You can't just focus on God loving you, rather you must look at God loving the world. He doesn't want anyone to perish but all to have eternal life with Him. God tells us in His Word that He first loved us, and we should love one another with His kind of love.

God's love is not about favor or getting rich. It's about His plan to save the world through Jesus and a relationship with us. One of the amazing things God consistently shows me is how much He loves people. When I pray for others, I feel the love of God deep within my heart that He feels toward that person. His love is so deep that I feel it's going to burst out of me. God wants to heal families from their broken hearts and from their sicknesses. He wants to remove all the pain Satan has caused, which is why he sent His son, Jesus Christ.

> *"The one who does what is sinful is of the devil, because the devil has been sinning from the beginning. The reason the Son of God appeared was to destroy the devil's works." 1 John 3:8*

SIN IN THE WORLD

The reason the world is so messed up is because of Satan and the sin that is committed in the world. Jesus came to destroy the devil's works. God did not cause sickness, death, heartache, and pain. These things were not experienced by Adam and Eve in the garden before they sinned. When you think about the nature of God, you will see mercy, grace, love, and compassion.

I hear many Christians talk about God's judgment, which is hard to explain.

Because of God's nature, judgment doesn't come as quickly as we might think. He is very patient and long-suffering to wait for people to turn to Him for help. Throughout the world, you can find God taking people the long way around to give them time to turn their hearts toward Him. When we look back at the story of Moses, He didn't immediately punish Egypt for the slavery of the Israelites. But with great mercy, He gave them numerous chances to let the Israelites go free.

In Jeremiah 12, Jeremiah is complaining to God about His justice. When people look for judgment, they are not looking at God's love toward people, but where is God's justice for them?

"You are always righteous, LORD, when I bring a case before you. Yet I would speak with you about your justice: Why does the way of the wicked prosper? Why do all the faithless live at ease? You have planted them, and they have taken root; they grow and bear fruit. You are always on their lips but far from their hearts. Yet you know me, LORD; you see me and test my thoughts about you. Drag them off like sheep to be butchered! Set them apart for the day of slaughter! How long will the land lie parched and the grass in every field be withered? Because those who live in it are wicked, the animals and birds have perished. Moreover, the people are saying, 'He will not see what happens to us.'" Jeremiah 12:1-4

Jeremiah is complaining to God about justice and wanting Him to destroy the wicked people in the land. Jeremiah is looking for God's justice to prove he is righteous, and they are wicked. The danger in thinking this way is that we all have sinned and have done wicked things. God has a perfect timing to accomplish His plan, but a part of that plan includes His mercy and grace.

As we go back into these stories about Moses, Joseph, and Paul, we will experience God's love, mercy, and grace to wicked people. Going against the current is not always about going down the tougher road but learning about why God sends the storms to direct us on His path. While many people are looking for justice, they are focused on the wrong thing. God answers Jeremiah in verse 5.

> *"If you have a raced with men on foot and they have worn you out, how can you compete with horses? If you stumble in safe country, how will you manage in the thickets by the Jordan?" Jeremiah 12:5*

God wants His people who are going toward His promises to not compete with men, but with horses. You were called to not hang out with the wicked, but to run along with God on the journey He has for you. So do not get frustrated in the process; it's not all about you, but rather God is trying to bring as many people to heaven as He can.

When I was running the half marathon, God spoke to my heart that I had finished running my own race, and it was now time to turn around and help someone else in theirs. When we are focused on ourselves in the race we must run, we miss out on the bigger picture that God is trying to accomplish. This moment in my life was a parallel of the journey God promised me. If I trusted God to turn around and go His way, I would get to the finish line.

GOD SHOWED HIS LOVE

How God set the Israelite people free wasn't the easiest or the quickest way to deliver them. It was God's way of loving Egypt by giving them mercy and grace. It also showed the Israelite people that God would protect them if they did what was right. When the plagues came against Egypt, they did not touch the Israelite people. God gave ten different plagues to test the heart of Pharaoh, but the plagues did not touch a single Israelite.

Pharaoh kept testing God by going after the Israelites, even in the desert. Just as justice came to Egypt at the Red Sea, God will bring justice to the world at a certain point. I believe God is going to bring a great move of Himself to the world, so they will know He is real and that He loves them. We are in a season where God is testing the hearts of people and seeing if they will cry out to Him for help.

When Joseph was sold into slavery by his brothers, then to Potiphar's house, and taken to prison, God was bringing Joseph closer to Pharaoh for the moment Pharoah would have the dreams. Even though this was hard on Joseph, God was showing His love to Egypt and the surrounding areas to provide food through the seven years of famine. He knew Egypt had the resources to gather enough grain for all the people during the seven years of abundance.

With Paul's story, even though he was in prison and was being transported by a ship to another prison, God was with him. He allowed a storm to blow against the ship, but God protected every man on this ship, even the wicked people who did not deserve it. God's love shows His mercy and not His judgment. He also allowed the ship to fall apart off the coast of Malta. He allowed Paul to be bitten by a snake, and when nothing happened to him, he was revered as a god. Rather than keep this attention on himself, Paul introduced them to the God of Israel by healing the sick and ministering to the hearts of the people.

DO NOT GIVE UP

Lastly, I want to encourage you not to give up. God has a plan and looks patiently for willing people to complete it with Him.

> *"Let us not become weary in doing good, for at the proper time we will reap a harvest if we do not give up." Galatians 6:9*

God is looking at the seed you're sowing. It's not good enough to just plow the field or plant, but we must not give up to reap the harvest. If we never reap the harvest, it will go to waste.

Let me pray for you:

Heavenly Father,

Thank You for the plan You have us in even though it may be very difficult to complete. I know we can do all things through Christ who gives us strength. Help us have a desire and determination to not give up and to keep putting one foot in front of the other. May we receive a harvest of souls with the plan You have given us. Help us with our weaknesses and let us get rid of our fears.

Your strength is like a rock under our feet. Let us learn to not make decisions from feelings and emotions but let us make those decisions from your peace, love, and joy. Everything we do, we do because of the love we have in our heart. Thank You. We do it all to give You glory, honor, and all praise for our lives.

Amen

ABOUT THE AUTHOR

Larry Hutcheson is passionate about sharing the good news of what a relationship with Jesus Christ can do in a person's life. He has dedicated his life to follow God's purpose for him and carry out that purpose even when it means walking out the unknown and live a life evident of God's love.

Larry has been married to his high school sweetheart, Shalene, since 1994. They have three beautiful daughters, pursuing God's purpose for their own lives. If Larry could sit down and chat with you, he would share his journey of walking out his yes for the Lord and that going against the current is always worth it.

LarryHutcheson.com

Made in the USA
Monee, IL
30 November 2023

47210853R00068